T0056705

Secular Eden

PARIS NOTEBOOKS 1994–2004

Secular Eden

PARIS NOTEBOOKS 1994–2004

Harry Clifton

WAKE FOREST UNIVERSITY PRESS

Published simultaneously in paperback
and in a clothbound edition
First North American Edition published 2007
Copyright © Harry Clifton

All rights reserved
For permission to reprint or
broadcast these poems, write to:
Wake Forest University Press
Post Office Box 7333
Winston-Salem
North Carolina 27109

Designed and composed by Quemadura
Typeset in Bank Gothic and Trinité

Printed in the United States of America

Library of Congress Card Number 2007931346
ISBN (clothbound): 978-1-930630-37-6
ISBN (paperback): 978-1-930630-36-9

Wake Forest University Press
www.wfu.edu/wfupress
Second Printing 2011

à Brigitte Fabre

The sky would have to be deep blue
To equal that dream, its wooden stairs
And landings, where you and I
Are arriving. She is not there,

Our hostess. But her high voice
Singing, feminine spirit
Invisible, ratifies this space.
Deep summer, early morning—

We sit on our baggage and wait.
Have they come, at last, to a stop,
Displacements, night-travels out of states
Not marked on any map?

Guardian angel, grant us the pity
Of backstairs lodgings, under a roof
Mansarded, in an old city
Cold as charity, warp and woof

Of marketplace and institute,
Body and soul, the North, the South
Archimedean, beyond dispute,
Locus of leverage, locus of truth.

Exhausted now, we would sleep
Anywhere. Will she not be back,
Our hostess? The key is in your keeping
She is telling us. Unpack

And pass, by miracle, through the door
To the brilliant kitchen, white and blue,
The shelves of books, the music scores,
All I have abandoned to you.

Feather-bedded, lie down here
And find your place in history.
Wanderers, after many years,
You are where you were meant to be.

CONTENTS

NOTEBOOK TWO

(PARIS, AUGUST 1997–MARCH 1999)

NOTEBOOK THREE

(PARIS–DUBLIN–PARIS, APRIL 1999–DECEMBER 1999)

NOTEBOOK FOUR

(PARIS–SYDNEY–PARIS, JANUARY 2000–DECEMBER 2002)

NOTEBOOK FIVE

(PARIS, AUGUST 2003–JUNE 2004)

The poems selected here are from five separate notebooks kept between June 1994 and September 2004. Gratitude is owed to the editors of many journals where they were first published, including *Poetry* (Chicago), *American Poetry Review, Southern Review, Stand, London Review of Books, Times Literary Supplement, Poetry Review* (UK), *Poetry Ireland Review, Irish Times, La Revue Atlantique, Poetes Irlandais du Xxieme siecle* (Verdier), *Forward Book of Poetry* 1997 and 1998, *Metre, The Recorder* (New York), *Princeton Library Chronicle, Thumbscrew, New Writing 9* (Penguin Books), *Leviathan Quarterly, Oxford Poetry, Backyards of Heaven* anthology (Canada), *Irish Review, Speaking from the Heart* (Constable), *Best Irish Poems 2007* (Southword), *Kore Broadsheet 10* (Trinity College), *Qualm* website. Eleven poems were published as a chapbook *God in France* by Metre Publications in 2002, and Wake Forest University Press published two poems in *The Wake Forest Series of Irish Poetry, 1* (2005).

Notebook One

PARIS–BORDEAUX–PARIS,

JUNE 1994–JULY 1997

WHEN THE PROMISED DAY ARRIVES

One golden day the whole of life contains —HOLDERLIN

When the promised day arrives
That prophets and old wives
Are always predicting, examine your hands
Where the fatelines have been read
And what you wanted to hear is said—
At last, you will understand.

The traffic, birds, pneumatic drills
Of an absolute city
Will be yours. White architecture,
Classical, and the sky a brilliant blue
In early winter, season of clarity,
Urban trains, their clean electric smell—
And the rest will be up to you

To do with as you please.
Ideal objects, the people, the trees,
Giving themselves unconsciously,
Fish and vegetable stalls, a splash of awnings
Everywhere, tobacco and coffee
Of student cafes, and the energies
Of expectation, for it is still morning

And the best is still to come.
The sizzle of meat

On skillets, chantilly and rum
In sawdust joints, where the officeworkers eat,
The prisoners of time.
And feeling it in you, the appetite

Afterwards, someone at any price—
Her sallow skin, her almond eyes,
Black hair, and cold professional zeal
Conducting you towards release,
The old, regressive peace
That was always better imagined than real,

Always unreachable.... Follow your own arc
Into decline, not all at once
But gradually. Battered shopfronts,
The immigrant quarter, littered with orange-peel,
Syringes, a ferris wheel
Stopped dead, your alter egos
Lounging at every corner, out of work,
Who dreamt, like you, of life in the ideal city.

You will take it all in
As expected; the golden afternoon,
The parks, the changing angle of light
On nave and transept, human futures and pasts.
You are not the first, you will not be the last

To follow your own shadow
As it lengthens. Dispassionate,
Steady your gaze. Already, it is late,

And the blue deepens, merciless and clear.
The unities fall into place.
Disillusionments, lost years

Are part of the story. The rest is praise—
Be equal to it, pay your way
With the same blank cheque that floats so many lives,
Your birthright, and your crossing fee,
When the promised day arrives.

DRÔLE DE GUERRE

1

All autumn, we rested
In villages, the evacuated space
That once was Alsace.
If the front moved west

It would roll us over,
Shame us, with looted bivouacs
We could never give back
To their owners. Our lovers,

Our families, were far away
In Paris. We could drink
Fine wine, on soldier's pay.
We had too much time to think.

Instead, from the skies
Came propaganda. 'Abstract man
Of the plutodemocracies!'
All of it began,

'You are digging your own graves!'
Quality paper, veined,
Calligraphic, falling like rain
In the shape of autumn leaves.

Our churches were swallows' nests—
Abandoned. Trench fear
Possessed us. Why were we here?
In the name of what discredited past,

What centuries, what hope?
Faithless since the age of twelve,
Were we to hang ourselves
With our own rope?

2

All winter, Alsace,
Our frozen allotropic state,
Anaesthetised us, cold and white—
The cold of liquefied gas.

Up they went, our weather balloons,
To steady themselves and veer
In the blue atmosphere
Below zero, the empty noons

We charted for invisible trends.
They would read them, the artillery,
And throw them away.
Was there nothing left to defend?

All winter, coming back from leave,
Foregathering at Café de la Gare,
We joked about the *drôle de guerre*
And spoke of Paris. 'Bereaved!

No lights, and the dancehalls cold
On the rue de Lappe.
And the women? Taken up
With children and the old....'

All winter, all winter—
Infidelities, censored out.
Feverish from our typhoid shots
We were cold at centre.

Cynical, the artillery
Salvoed into a blue void,
That our morale not be destroyed,
That we felt ourselves free.

3

Now, at last, it is Spring.
A schoolteacher, with his pipe
And his sergeants' stripes,
Works the 'phones. The wires sing

With rumours. There will be Peace.
The War will last ten years.
Tomorrow, we move to the rear.
Democracies to the North and East

Have fallen already, in lightning campaigns.
Shocktroops, one metallic flood,
Are pouring through in brotherhood,
Unthinking unison, holy disdain

'From which we have so much to learn'
De Courcy tells me, as he stalls,
Unzips his fly, on children's dolls.
Now, they say, it is our turn,

And the villages of Alsace,
Platonic recollections
Of childhood, whiten, regress,
As we speed in the wrong direction,

Squaddies in jeeps. Throw away
Clausewitz On War.
Today, you would profit more
From the jokes in Le Canard Enchainé.

Tomorrow, we put to the test
Europe, our glory and our shame,
For the millionth time
As the fight moves west.

WHITE RUSSIANS

White Russians at Renault's works ... no doubt they invented for
themselves readymade pasts and illusive futures. —SIMONE WEIL

I scan them, floor by floor, the lists of names—
Champy, Coudert, Floras, Garnier.
Van Ronsele—where did he come from?
Klein, our resident German—prisoner or refugee?
Fellow tenants, footsteps on the stairs
That smell of beeswax, voices behind doors,
Presences, through the ceilings and the floors
Of arrondissement twelve. What exiles? What despairs?
Lair-Ferreira? Crossing the Pyrenees
    From the Spanish Civil War?
Lazarevitch, of course, and you and me.

Lazarevitch? Blue, in his Renault fatigues,
Among white-hot bobbins, armatures
For the trams and metros, pieceworkers leagued
Against bosses, slaving like Stakhanovites,
Four hundred, eight hundred, twelve hundred pieces an hour,
To beat the quota. Mensheviks, old Whites,
The ciphers of exile. Back behind the Urals
Russia outshouts them, with her millionfold refrain—
At Vladivostok, the Sea of Japan froze.
    Our clothes rattled like tin.
For fear of gangrene, we amputated our toes.

Inventing victories, glossing over defeats,
Avoiding each other on the Paris streets,
Kicking over the tables, screaming 'I!'
At the goddess of history, lodged in the pigsties
Of Issy, Malakoff and Porte Saint Cloud,
Black with factory smoke, and the thunder of trains
Through fractured glass, alone in every crowd,
Asleep in the metro, asleep along the Seine—
White Russians in exile . . . Ruthless, the hiring clerk,
    At dawn, at the Renault works
Chooses his women, feeds his assembly lines.

Lev Isaakovitch Schwarzmann, alias Shestov,
Tsvetayeva, Sergei Efron, Weil—
Double agents, poets and impostors,
Dostoyevskian children, weighing on a scale
That factory of Renault, against one innocent tear.
At six, the blue trapeze door wheezes open.
Steelworkers enter, link themselves to the chain
Of cold necessity. What about Perekop?
Or the Camp of Swans? Who remembers now, who cares
    Which side, if any, you were on?
Lazarevitch? A name on the fifteenth floor,

Indifferent as Paris. . . . Sellier, Langlois,
Senecaux, Fabre. What about Le Bigot?
Who was he? And what about you? And what about me?
Once upon a time there were Green intrigues
And goings into exile. . . . *John McBride, are you there?*

Oblivion answers, silence on the stairs,
Our neighbours shuffling about, in the in-between
Of rented space, their coffee, their Gitanes,
Like fumes of sublimation in the air.
Someday, when we all have time to spare
    From dreaming the future,
Re-imagine the past, how I came to be here.

Fetching up in Paris, nothing better to do,
I stroll the streets, relive the old campaigns—
The mud of Brunswick, snowy plains
Around Smolensk, where we, the dandified retinue
Of Napoleon, watched our soldiers freeze,
Broke rank, ourselves became refugees.
The *alimentaires*, the merchants of fine champagne,

Their magnums in the windows, mock my impoverished state,
At forty a failure, wormwood in my toasts,
And the risk, perhaps, of alienating my hosts—
To middle age, to social disrepute,
To absolute honesty, and the pleasures that pass
Backstairs, that everyone knows about,
No-one mentions . . . To the crash of breaking glass

And the cry 'Rattrappez-le! II me doit cent francs!'
That marks the end of our Utopia,
My socialist friends. We broke the bank
Of Revolution, hung our hopes
On Comedie actresses, with their makeup cracked.
Between their legs the cities we sacked—
A vision of injured bleeding, after the act.

War, succession, strung like a narrative thread
Through static time . . . Who knows, when I am dead,
Perhaps they will read me properly. Only then,

In Nineteen Thirty, or Two Thousand and Ten,
When the ball has been unmasked, and the inhibitions shed,
Will the terrible truth sink in.
Meanwhile, rabbit stew and a bottle of red,

Hotel de Bruxelles, and the rue de Richelieu,
The Life of Henri Brulard, me or you,
And lending my name, or my millionth pseudonym,
To the universal mood—
That happiness was fought for, happiness denied
In time of icons, pieties and hymns—
Death the only terror. For there never was a God.

AUXERRE 1969

1

In the mornings, a bowl of milky coffee—
I shook hands with everyone.

No matter that the night before
Their rough red wine had loosened my tongue

For the first time in years. New day, new world—
Let us all introduce ourselves.

Afterwards, walking the shadowless streets,
From my eyes the scales were falling—

A blaze of primary colour. Depthless blue
Fanned my cheeks, but the air was still cool—

I was sixteen, on my way to school,
A stammerer in the tongue of romance.

Around me, with their unbound hair,
Were the fabulous daughters of France.

2

Afternoon heat. We were under the trees,
Undressing. She was fifteen,

A woman already. Her rippled thighs
Slipped waistdeep into the river, ahead of me,

And we joined the others, in the strong current,
The Yonne, translucent and green,

Flowing through us, I know not where
To this day, whether in or around Auxerre,

Whether history or the biological surge
That swept us off our feet and gave us our heads.

Was it the same river
The old men dapped, beneath the cathedral—

Giant rods and infinitesimal fish?
I remember them now, but they are all dead.

3

At night, in the moonlight,
Brown mice clung to the yellow walls of the house—

My spots of time. We were back early
From the country dance. A man had bent her in half,

Madame Monnier, in the heat of a foxtrot.
She still wore a look of outrage.

Lusts, the pinpricks on my flesh,
Stung like mosquitoes. I was still chaste,

Awake in the darkness, with the moon outside
About to be conquered, and the barricades

Going up in my own home country.
A refugee from domestic wars,

I bore within me invisible scars.
My tongue was still tied.

It was a closed space. From the moment I saw it
I knew I could depend on it.
To hell with the endless weathers
Passing above, and the high apartments
Shadowing it. Down here
On the stone bench, of an autumn morning,
I felt, for a moment, the heat of sun on my face
As it angled around the corner
Out of sight. My patch of sky
Went blue then, or grey,
And I went inside.
                          But it was always there,
The garden. At its centre
A tree, a plum tree
As I discovered, when the bluish fruit
Appeared through the leaves in September,
Gave it core, and strength, and definition.
Yellow courgettes, and ripening tomatoes
Bound to their splints. And tough carnations
Half in love with the wire that fenced them in.
And the clay, of course, rich and black
After rain, or a dry brown bath
For thrushes and sparrows.
And day after day, the same man
Clearing weeds, or laying a path
According to some unspecified plan.

No need to mention where all this was.
I had travelled enough, by then,
To dispense with where. Sufficient to say
A horse's tail appeared, one day,
Above a gable, or a streak of cirrus—
Time and the future, far away.
Woodsmoke, the waft of cooking,
Brought me back to earth—
I was here, in the garden. An old woman
With green fingers, fed me generic names
Like Flower, or Tree,
As if nothing else mattered
But the garden, and having your own key.

REDUCTIO

*I could spend the rest of my life simply drawing a table
and two chairs.* —ALBERTO GIACOMETTI

What is big? What is extended in space?
Not this studio, surely, not this glass
On a wooden table, or the apple
Trapped forever in the intersecting planes
Of redemptive vision. Certainly not this face—
But the rue d'Alesia, outside in the rain,
The millions of strange people
Whirled like atoms through the hub of Montparnasse

As night comes down, and the lit conceptual cages,
Dome, Select, Rotonde, the stamping-grounds
Of seeing and being seen, the gilt cafés
And mirrored brothels of the rue de l'Echaudee,
Where goddesses file naked on the stage,
Invite appraisal, and your mind's hot foundry
Casts them in bronze, remote as steles,
Cycladic or Sumerian, ancestral but still real.

What is big? What is extended in space?
Not the little tin soldiers, oh so small
In toyshop windows, though they say it all.
Not the yellow decals, not the pedestrian lights,
Stationary Man, or Walking Man, in the night's

Electric statuary. Not the living gaze
Forever fugitive, but only the skull,
The pleasure-seekers after hours, crashed out

On benches and late metros, heads agape
In a staring void. 'All the living are dead'
It suddenly hits you. No, not Woman now, not Tree—
And where did it get you, that theft of bread
In childhood? Not Paris now, but infinities
Of disconnected people, faces, times,
Humanity dissolving into shapes
At the ends of avenues, at the ends of rhymes.

What is big now? What is extended in space?
A single tungsten bulb, a Palace-at-Four,
Your lean-to shed. Inside it, memory swarms
With ancient heads, in the depths of revolving doors
Beheld, forgotten.... From table to wooden chair
Saharas spread. A glass suspended in air—
You take a drink. To keep your fingers warm
You busy yourself, with the one loved face
Attempted endlessly, with the one loved form.

I can't go on. I'll go on. —SAMUEL BECKETT, *The Unnameable*

As I staggered into the rue du Bac
The heavens opened. In the zinc bars
Drinkers paused. Outside, police
Took shelter in nearby doors,
And I thought of Giacometti,
Legless on a mantelpiece,
Or Beckett's talking head in a jar,

Who would give the best of themselves
For an hour of conversation,
A blue streak, an unstoppable jag,
Incontinent, shattering
Plateglass windows, Sèvres delph,
Like a man on a drunken batter.
Metros spun their monologues

Underground. I closed my eyes
A moment, to clear my head
Of vodka and foie gras,
Of oysters bedded in ice,
And heard the swish of Michelin treads,
The bicycles, stilettos pass.
And blinked again. I was not dead,

Just following the curve of the world
In my own small way,
Rambling on, with nothing to say,
From shelter to shelter. Soon, a *quai*
Would show itself, round the next bend.
For no good reason, pretty girls
And the stone statue of Chateaubriand

Leapt, like improvisation,
Into the picture. Pedalling
Hard, another Molloy
Downwind of his destination,
Dressed in dickybow, held an umbrella
Overhead, as he wobbled away.
Our Lady of the Miraculous Medal,

Chimed, just once. I saw, I heard,
At the heart of desperate cheerfulness,
Not Spirit, not the Word,
But winking neon, blues and greens,
A brilliant pharmaceutical cross,
The tricorned hats of Etamine's,
The profit and the loss.

And suddenly, there it was, the Seine—
A street the length of a cloudburst
Or a song on an underground train
From station to station, falling away
To the dry heaves, to yellow bile,
To the cold water of rainswept *quais*.
Bloodshot from a night on the tiles,

Others besides myself, in straits,
Were waiting for the skies to break,
And whistling in the dark—
Alcoholics with the shakes,
Bearded tramps, their flies undone,
Accusing heaven. Early or late?
I no longer knew. But I had to go on.

That Schnittke quartet ... Let me hear it again
If the tape still works. A slow start,
Faraway chords—or is it the dust and static
Travelling, in my Sony, even further
Than these disembodied sounds
Out of Russia, the pluckings,
The pizzicatos, the mad mazurkas
Shot through with sadness, the great sadness
Of northern plains, of freezing skies
Unceasingly grey, for months on end,
Of wooden cattle-barns collapsed on themselves
And silver birches, lining the road
To the horizon. ... ?
                              That was the first time—
And I listen again, more carefully.
Invisible fingers, plucking imaginary chords.
Coldness, depth. Great spaces,
None of them physical. I am here,
Alone, in the warmth of another kitchen,
And for all I know, the baking fish,
The steamed potatoes, the blue and white tiles
Snug as a Russian stove, to while away
Winter in, my seventh winter
Of apprenticeship, might be telling me
To let go at last, to be free. A drizzle of violins—
Or is it the batteries bleeding?
A snow of quotations, ironic of course,

From the fathers of harmony,
Melting, melting away
To everyday chaos, and through it a phone
Insistently ringing, a sound from another world—
My long distance call. I knew I was waiting for something.

BARE ARM

When the blind goes up
In the morning, one bare arm,
A woman's, from the dormer
Opposite, swims up

To the surface of her life
And turns away,
A mother, a housewife,
To the depths of her own day,

And the skies flow past,
And the silvered glass
Reflects them, her window
No one can see into,

Except, one night
Of sultry weather,
Energies, stray lightnings,
We glimpsed each other

Naked, in the small hours,
Coming from showers
And lovemaking, two spouses
In opposite houses

Pausing, in the lit frame
Of revelation,
Not knowing each other's name,
Uncaring, unconditional

For once, two creatures
Awake, while everyone slept,
Alive in the forest
Of second nature.

With your white flesh and dark mind
How northern you are, my wife,
To be coming into these latitudes
I am familiar with. Long before birth
I learnt it, the dance of attitudes
That passes, here, for social life—
The fertile plains, the shadowless earth
Of happiness, with the dark side
Filtered out, forever denied.
Appearances . . . But you defined
The lie of the south, and cut like a knife
Through art, physique and platitude,
With your white flesh, and your dark mind.

At three on a winter afternoon
You reached out blindly, and snapped on the lamp,

And I saw, suddenly, how late it was
To be having this conversation. A streak of light

As thin as the minute-hand of a solar clock
Burned its way over the floor

From the great outdoors,
And for a moment, we hung in the middle realm

Between day and night. 'This envelope'
You said, as you folded it twice for luck,

'Imagine it, as the shape of a human spine
In the earliest week. . . .' And I saw it, an embryo

Setting out blindly, our mythic lines
Foreclosing around it, as the ancestors

Hovered, the living and the dead.
A million selves were crowding to a head

Inside me, each with its separate hope
Of not being nothing. And the unsaid

Broke through, with 'How many years have we left?'
As that brilliant spoke of the sun

Shifted its allegiance, and was gone,
And the minute-hand moved on

For ever and ever. And over the floor
It spread, like something foretold—

The thinnest end of the wedge
Of absolute darkness, and of absolute cold.

When a man strays out of his private sphere
As you did, wandering the cold halls
Of Stockholm at ungodly hours,
Telling himself forever that duty calls,

When any normal man would still be in bed
Or crying Eureka! warm on a Dutch stove,
His best work is behind him, and ahead
Only eminence, good behaviour,

A self reconstructed from the inside out
To dignify the early morning whims
Of a northern Queen, who bowdlerises hymns

At the top of her voice, proclaims herself Saved,
And leaves you to your Philosophic Doubt,
Your wine and tobacco cures, and your thankless grave.

I went again, from the country of flux,
   To the country of still waters.
An old stone house, a mother and two daughters
Laying the same ghost, unweaving the hex
Like retted flax. To have loved, to have hated—
Now, to watch the nettles at the gate,
The harbingers of desertion, stand and wait,
Indigenous, for all of us to die out.

The book of invasions shuts itself, and the powers
   Throw open their great houses
Once and for all. Admire their jugs, glazed ewers,
Untouchable, frozen in time. And the blunderbuss
On the mantelpiece, and the harpsichord
In the drawing-room. Stables and pigsties,
Servants' quarters. Gravel in the yard,
A whitewashed front. Admire it and do otherwise

For the workhouse slate is wiping itself clean,
   Finality reigns,
And every victim, every breaker of stone
Stands like a monument, now, to his own pain.
The Indian meal, the quart of buttermilk
In a tin mug, the dish on the spellbound table,
Numinous, its every grain unspilt,
Accounts for itself, in the completed fable.

Hurt consciousness, dazedly seeking out water
　　Maidenhead, luckless in love,
Now, second childhood. Mother, is it over
For the cloven halves of the apple, both your daughters?
Father, in your otherworld of quiet,
Where the great gentleness reigns, beyond spite
Or envy, higher than theodolite
Or spirit-level, tell me, do the grouse turn white

On the winter mountains? Now, you finally know,
　　And the chain of expiation
Breaks forever. A pub, a filling station
In the wilderness. I park my car and go
On foot up an empty valley. Signs of habitation
Once, long ago. On ruined sills, a wren,
Territorial, marks its spaces out.
In the riverbed, a skitter of ghostly trout—

And there it is again, in all its flux,
　　My country of still waters.
Racing light and shadow, mossgrown alders
Overhanging a waterfall. Sheep, transfixed
Or fleeing. Water, wood and stone,
A lost inheritance, physical, entire,
Disentangling itself from barbed wire,
Ridding itself of history, coming into its own.

The twenty-second Sunday in Ordinary Time—
   A chalice is raised
To Spirit in Matter. Silence, a chime,
While half the country bows its head and prays.
No past, no future. Stillness, a moratorium
Pausing over the mother and the daughters,
The old stone house, the country of still waters,
Wherever it may be, whenever it happens to come.

SHEEPFOLD

Fleeing the Ice Age, sheep converge
On the only human being for miles around

Who happens to be me. Their expectations
Are narrow and pure. To hear an absolute Word

In this Babel of valley-sounds, that cancels out
Skulls in streambeds, ribcages in heather

Pecked by carrion crow. And the interim judgements
Of August, the shears and branding-irons,

The crowded pens, the stained fleece falling away
Like overcoats, bartered to the world as it is

That abandons them, to the north and the east wind
High in this beyond, where our shadows cross.

Am I man or angel, playing God
Each seventh day, with a super-intelligent dog?

They make sheep's eyes at me, their theologian,
Chewing his stalk of feather-grass. Their tongues

Hang out like patients, for a fluoridated dose
Against oblivion, nothingness, the cold.

Mist and blanket bog, where the ice sheets vanished.
But it is here, according to the books,
Cloudberry is to be found—
In a single patch, up the wild Glenelly valley.
I can see you looking at me
As if to say 'What? In this weather?
Are rosehips reddening haws and deadly nightshade
Not enough for you? Poisons, panaceas
Bursting from the hedges
Of half the country?'

Call it bakeapple, for all I care,
As the Canadians do. Alps and tundras,
Bogs and blasted heaths, are its chosen ground.
As for me, I'm tired of life reduced
To a household metaphor. . . .
                                        I want to go back
Just once, behind all that is Ireland,
To the age of free migrations
Where a man sets out, with only a Word in his head
And the needle of a shattered compass
Guiding him, through what is now no more than landscape,
With its huddle of frightened sheep
In driving westerlies, blown bog-cotton
Trembling like the beards of a million prophets

Leading their chosen peoples out of exile—
To eat of the tasteless fruit
Of universality, rooted
Like myself, in the invisible,
And belonging everywhere.

All the way south, there was only this road
Twisting through the mountains
To Siena and beyond. A sanded track
Beaten flat by pilgrimage,
Littered with axles, broken felloes,
Endings. Flooded
Out of season, losing itself,
Re-appearing, in the moon-landscape
Of the Alpine foothills
Ghastly with mile-high silence, unbroken
But for bird-caw and rockfall—
And suddenly the olives, silver-grey,
And the true south starting.
                              In the distance
Siena, allegorical,
Dreamed of before ever met with,
Shimmered before us. Then, the long approach
Between sanded tumuli, the feminine swells
Of the Tuscan hills, with the factions
Perched in their hawks' nests
Jealously watching, and the skies
Ever bluer, the heat increasing,
And Paris, from where we had started,
So far behind us,
In a space measured only by footfalls.

Through the North Gate we entered,
To a pride of spires,

Fine counting-houses, streets full of rats
Big enough to feed on
In siege-time. Vain women, vain men,
With a preference for red
Like their painters. Coinage, stamped
With the she-wolf, stolen from Rome.
A delicate skein of allegiances
Quivering, unspoken,
On every breeze. The Romans, the French;
To the east, the Florentines;
North, on the pilgrim route from Augsburg
Through the mountains, the Emperor on the move
With his flaxen-haired soldiers. . . .

                          Autumn—
From tree to tree the mist-nets spread
For migrant birds, and the nets on the ground
For olives. Venison, game, good wine—
Winter and Spring, we lived in that ideal,
Under the sign of gluttony, science, art,
Then started north, with the road still open,
And the skirmishes, out to sea,
Already visible. Over our shoulders
Siena, dwindling, still could be seen
When the first buboes purpled us.
By the mountains, in the ghastly foothills,
Our dead, unburied, swelled and burst
At every turn. How many rats
Were travelling with us, anyone might guess,
But that we were carriers
No one doubted—plague spots on our faces,
In our pockets, new cosmogonies.

STAGGERING ASHORE

Staggering ashore, on Prospero's island,
Making a landfall in Twelfth Night,
Illyria, or the coast of Ireland
Caught, I would be indicted,

So, as usual, the disguise
Before striking inland.
But how will I be recognized
And who will understand

That I am brother to my sister,
Son, or rightful heir?
Malvolio, the ill-wisher,
Lurks under every stair,

And Caliban, in the marram grass
Of Booterstown sloblands
Sticks in the mud of drunkenness,
Old stay-at-home, old rainy day friend.

Minor angels, minor demons
Whiz like irritants round my ears—
Voices, the shadows of peers,
The images of women

Coming near, unclasping hooks
In bedrooms, keeping the tragic
At bay; and the drowned books
Rising, to work hidden magic

On whatever isle this be.
I start to recognise the place—
Pigeon House, the Irish Sea,
Foghorns, an industrial haze,

And then, the mythic hinterland
Where fathers and daughters
Kiss goodbye, and the husband
Walks on charmed waters

To the marriage. Years before,
I had lost a home here, found a wife
Sequestered, where I swam ashore
From the old, shipwrecked life.

Chenier, in the state prison,
Waits for judgement. Today
As usual, the axe
Hangs over everyone,
But the sounds from the courtyard
Are normal. Women washing
In the grey dawn, their hour
Of air and exercise,
The ribaldries of prostitutes,
The sobs of the wellbred
Mending their tatters.
Fate, not politics,
Is what jailed them here,
But for now, they go on living.

Audible snores. The prison clerk
Snoozing over his ledger
Two doors down. The guards
In their iron cage
Playing cards. The Queen
Can be heard through the walls
As always, praying
To the ghost of her old religion—
As if it would save her! Anywhere else
It would be the same—
Inside, outside,
Far away, tucked up at home
Or clattering through the thoroughfares
Under the doom, the Terror.

Common keeps, and abbatoir straw—
Above, the special hells
Of privileged cells. An iron door opens
Two floors down
In deathly silence. You, you and you
For tunic and shaved nape,
The axe, the block. Chenier,
Held on conspiracy,
Listens, as the hubbub
Rises again, and the hot air
Wafts their childishness
Up from below; the bright balloons
Bubbling through the bars,
The screams of laissez-faire.

The nave and transept, sandblasted clean,
Of an empty church on remembrance day.
Sacred still? Deconsecrated?
Hard to know. He had noticed her
Immediately, a daughter of good family,
Chestnut hair, and the loose expensive clothes
That hid an exquisite body,
Strolling about, between huddles of elderly nuns
And drunks asleep in the back pews—
One of the post-religious, like himself.

On the walls, the scrapings of old frescoes,
Peeling mass-times from another age,
And the tasteless splendour
Of painted angels, plaster saints
Collapsing . . .
                    At a side-altar
She was kneeling now, in the heat of penny candles,
Forehead kissing the bare stone floor,
Hands imploring. And her fabulous hair
That could have washed the feet of Christ
Had he really existed, flung in sheaves before her.
Minutes passed. He went on watching,
He, who had mentally undressed her—
Embarrassed now, at misjudgement,
Intrusion. At her Absolute nakedness.

It was always there, the gaze of the other,
Interpenetrating his days
Wherever he went. What price now
The women of rue Sud Est
In a bitter wind, their naked breasts
Blue with the cold, their three-forked tongue
Of blow-ins, illegals, making a *sou*
On borrowed beds?
                    All that was dead—
The scenery changed to a few furnished rooms
And a pair of eyes that followed him everywhere,
Inside or out. Possessiveness?
Love? There was nothing to choose.
A contact lens dropped into her shoe
At nightfall, and ground itself underfoot.

Still, there was the consolation of books.
At a rough guess, hundreds—
Sublimated worlds, with their spines all broken
And their story told. *Desire*
Roams infinite streets
Until, one day, it meets the desires of another....

A cough in the kitchen. Scrape of a chair
On a tiled floor. Herself in there
Forever creating order. And the regular beat
Of clock and heart, as the short-changed body

Lived its sentence out
And died its death.
                    Before that, throwbacks—
To be seen off, at the top of a spiral stairs,
To clatter downwards, deaf to himself
And his own deepening echoes,
Stairwell upon stairwell, shade upon shade,
Passing, repassing, unable to rest
Except in the blink of an eye on rue Sud Est—
To look back up, from the hothouse hells
Of the erotically damned,
Impossibly far down, and to see her there.

MAYDAY

But when the melancholy fit shall fall
Sudden from heaven like a weeping cloud
—JOHN KEATS

I stumbled up to bed at one a.m.
The worse for a couple of whiskies. Woke at ten

With the silence everywhere, that deepest of peace
Unfelt in ages. Now for the yellow house

Across the street, for the greening trees in the square,
For my clearheaded grasp of blade and kitchenware—

Mind over matter. For the Here, the Now,
For fruit and coffee, for a reincarnate Thou

To pour myself into! For grapes, for wheat
On threshold and lintel, the sound of running feet

Out there on the pavement, along the cathedral close
As a rainshower passes . . . There it goes

This first May morning, swallowed up in the spore-drift
Of ordinariness, and the roar of the day-shift.

THE HOUSE OF PIERRE LOTI

Now that the times of travel and writing are over
And a cuckoo calls across the estuary
Like an epilogue, and nothing is left to discover,
Exotic or banal, on land or sea,

That hasn't already been hung like a tapestry
In his fabulous rooms, or spun like yarn
As long as the ropemakers' sheds in the Admiralty,
Or said goodbye to, or welcomed on its return,

Let us honour the empty house of Pierre Loti
Who went by so many names, so many disguises,
Occident, Orient, anything to get free

Of second childhood, staring death in the face,
His whitewashed walls around him like horizons
Closing in on the old illusion—space.

She plied me with her tannic wine, champagne
That ages bitterly, as a harpsichord
Crashed out tangos, and the January rain
Rattled in off the grey Atlantic seaboard
West of Bordeaux. High were her windowpanes—
Eighteenth century. Speechless, she looked at me
As I sat beneath the artificial palm
At her dining-table, where others had sat before me,
For she was a woman on the wrong side of forty

Playing her wild cards. 'Strange, but he died of AIDS'
She said of the frenzied harpsichord player,
And I thought of Algeriennes, and the rough trade
Stubbing out cigarettes behind the place Saint Pierre,
Covert dealings, boredom of shoreleave days.
'Borges hated tangos—*trop vulgaire,*
Le sexe, la nostalgie, la vie des immigrés'
She went on speaking. Not that I cared
For all I could see was wide hispanic space,

Anterior life, the darkness of origins
Crowding in upon me, way back when.
'Esta noche mi emborracho bien'
Someone was singing. Old as original sin
Laura Monserrat floated, Maria la Vasca—
Female archetypes. Ostlers, muleteers,
Grandad out from Europe, still a clerk
At the turn of the century, shuffled like steers
Through the dance academies, round behind the abbatoir

Of Buenos Aires. '*Una calle in Barracas al Sud,*
Una noche in verano . . .' someone else sang,
And I heard, once and for all, the shutters clang
On the hour of conception. Mulatto blood
Raced like yellow fever in my veins—
Would she even notice? The South, the West,
The high cold of the Andes, white as a mother's breast
I never got close to . . . Vanished time regained—
It called itself South America, New Spain.

'Listen to this—*Les Blasons du Corps Féminin*'
She read from her sixteenth-century Pléiades
In a goldbound volume. 'Listen!—*petit connin*
Plus riche que les toisons du Colchos . . .' Jason's fleece
Was seated here in front of me! Here we had docked
That very afternoon, in the yellow light of a storm
Turning the Bordeaux bourgeois skyline black
With anticipations, electrical tinglings—
Here, where so many had left to try their luck

Were endings, beginnings. *Casas viejas!* Who
Were the women Europe failed, who stared
In tremendous mirrors, fingering first grey hairs?
I reached across and took her hands in mine,
And prayed to Mascarpillo, El Cachafaz,
At the shadow end of the transatlantic line—
Ghostly *compadritos*, shoeshine boys
Come up in the world, to harpsichords and hock,
Swerving their women in circles, against the clock.

TO WHOM IT MAY CONCERN

Whoever rents these rooms
Will be living under a waterfall

Of opened taps and telephone calls,
The whipcrack and the boom

Of sheets shaken out at dawn
From the floors above.

It will not do to be withdrawn.
It will not be enough

To bring a stranger to bed
Or say hello, on the public stairs,

To a woman not all there,
A man who might as well be dead.

It would help, before making the move,
To be stone-deaf, madly in love.

GOD IN FRANCE

I would like to be God in France, where no one believes anymore.
No calls on me, I could sit all day in cafes… —SAUL BELLOW

Allah of Islam! Yahweh of the Jews!
   They were calling upon me
All over Paris. Sabbaths, but the Bon Dieu
Had gone missing. I had set myself free
From Friday at the mosque, that pile of shoes,
Those thousands praying, Saturday Torah scrolls
And lit menorahs, Sundays salvaging souls—
From Daubenton, Des Rosiers, Saint Gervais,
To live again in the body, *l'homme moyen sensuel*

Adrift on the everyday. Streetlife, glass cafés
   Were my chosen ground.
Whatever I needed easily could be found
In a few square miles. Massage, phlebotomy,
Thalassal brines and hydrotherapeutics,
Mont Sainte Genevieve, with its hermeneutics,
Clichy for hardcore, all the highs and lows
Of pure *bien-etre*, like a bird in the hand.
Oh yes, if I wanted a woman, I knew where to go—

And who could deny me? Human, all my horizons
   Were reachable by train
From Austerlitz, Saint Lazare, the Gare de Lyon—
Not that I needed them. Gifted, like Urizen,

With omnipresence, simultaneity,
I could sit here over dinner, and still see
Normandy's apple-belt, or the lightwaves of the South
Collapsing on beaches. None could deny me
The springtime glitter of shad in the rivermouth

Of the long Garonne—that exquisite flesh,
   The bone that sticks in the throats
Of twenty centuries. Ichthyus the fish,
Like Renan's Christ, was dying, dying out
In the boredom of villages, of Proustian spires,
Provincial time, the echo-sounding fleets
Off La Rochelle, the sleep of the Loire,
The happiness that is almost too complete,
The Sunday afternoons that run on Michelin tyres.

Was that terrible? Tell me, was that sad?
   The night of the gods,
Of absences, abscondings, abdications?
Was I to kneel before him, the tramp at the station,
Unpeel his stinking trainers, wash his feet,
Amaze the wage-slaves? In the name of what
Would I drive the midnight circle of philosophers
Out of their TV studios, swivel chairs,
With hempen fire, the rope of castigation?

No. Instead I would sit here, I would wait—
   A dinner, a *café crème*,
A chaser of grog. Whatever else, there was time—
Let Judgement take care of itself. To celebrate—

That was the one imperative. Randomness, flux,
Drew themselves about me as I ate,
Protected by the nearnesses of women, their sex
Blown sheer through summer dresses, loving my food,
My freedom, as they say a man should.

The clouds of Ireland gathered over France—
Flights of swallows, blowing hot and cold
In their own force-fields, and the weightless dance
Of insects before rain. Our life on hold
Looked either way. The chairs, the groaning board
Littered with its aftermaths of feasts,
Were dragged indoors. A year or two, a third,
Was added, unaccountably, to the lease
Running out on the garden. Fifteen degrees
On the tapped barometer. We had drifted north
Just sitting there, just talking—cherry trees,
Excuses for a summer, used-up earth,
Our one-step-forward-two-steps-back advance,
And the clouds of Ireland, gathering over France.

THREE LOVE POEMS

1. THE SCARF

The automatic doors are sighing shut—
Be quick, decide! Your blue diaphanous scarf
Has freed itself of you. For an instant, it floats
Inside the carriage, on a wayward draught.
And suddenly you're gone. The platform clears.
Don't panic. Reason. Surely if I wait
In the one spot, you will find your way back here?
But for how long? And who has the keys
If we lose each other? Who has the house?
Who can find their way back, through time and space?
Up ahead of me, at some other station,
Re-united with your living soul,
Blue, diaphanous, free, you're past Control.
We should talk about what to do in these situations.

2. STEPS

I would know you by your footsteps anywhere—
If, tomorrow, I was struck blind
And had to listen, in streets and corridors,
To the million feet in passing, to the sounds
Separating themselves, in casual conversations,
Snatches of laughter, jazz and hurly-burly,
Pandemoniums, and orchestrations,
Yours would be under them, making your way through the world.

Hesitant, nervous, now you start, now stop—
Don't trip over your shadow or drown in the river!
Blind though I am, I can make you up
As you go along, approaching me forever
On Achilles' heels of instinct or change,
Out of the otherworldly, out of the strange.

3. ANOTHER KIND OF SLEEP

Another kind of sleep
Possesses us now. Mid-morning—
In the abandoned sink
A waterdrip. Sunken plates
And food that will not keep
Must wait, must wait.
Of the day's earnings,
Forfeited, try not to think.

A green, translucent ocean
Of medicines and lotions
On the night-table. Breath
Steady, the telephone
Out of its depth,
The mind, the body at one.

THE CAVE

'Let us ignore, for a moment,
The birth of Christ, as if that mattered
On the great scale of approximation
Where thousands of years
Mean nothing, and divine love,
If it ever existed, was a spark
In primordial dark,
Forgotten. Technique, of course—
We can talk about that,
But the rest is speculation.
Let us descend. . . .'
                              Spring forests
Closing overhead, a flight of stairs
Downward, to an iron door
In the earthface. And a lizard
Trapped, half-in, half-out,
Abandoning its severed tail
On the nether side
Of Creation, squeezing through
To the end of the Christian timescale.

'Disinfect the soles of your shoes
In the chlorine bath
Before you. Mind your head
On the alkaline shelf
Where groundwater gathers
Into stalactites. Yellows, reds,

A bison herd, a neolithic deer,
And signs, like noughts and crosses,
Beautiful, but meaningless
After all these years—
And here where ancient butter
Failed, a lamp may once have guttered
And gone out. . . .'
                    It was the boys,
They say, destroyed the original site,
Bursting in, all innocence,
That afternoon in 'Forty Four
While the war to end all wars
Was finishing. Chalkstream denizens
Of the Val de Vézère,
They must be old men now,
Still driving, saying their prayers
In the realm of troglodytes
And fossil fuels, up there
Where nobody knows it is night.

THE HOUSE OF THE DEPORTEE

Always in shadow, the house of the deportee
Planted its own landmark
On the avenue. Groceries, carparks
Owed their lives to him, who was taken away,

Bewitching himself to a tree at his own front door,
And in April, the spores,
Like mattress ticking, feathers that flew,
Swarmed at the windows hindsight could see through.

Not that the house was empty. Upstairs light,
Diurnal time, and the shapes
Of daily living—sudden figures of eight
And vague daguerreotypes

From the age of black and white
Against the shades. November, and at night,
While the asphalt smoked
With rain and the sizzling wakes

Of passing cars, the immigrant quarter slept
Behind double locks, iron shutters.
There, where trading hours were never kept,
Where the laws were lived in spirit, not in letter,

Where brilliant ilfachromes,
Household idylls, plastered the city gates,
They still remembered the man who got up from his plate
To answer a doorbell once, and never came home.

Theft of a leather jacket, fifty francs
And a set of keys. Report it at the desk—
No need for police, no need for the local bank
To change our in-code. Little risk
In a city of millions, in the small hours,
Of the ultimate stranger, the thief in the night,
A wandering moonbeam, highlights in his hair,
Suddenly standing before us, like a fright
Or an apparition, killing for metro fare
Or conscience money, chemicals or food,
For sexual favours, anything we share,
Loving each other, dealing in stolen goods.

THE WHITE WINE LANDSCAPE

for Angela Madden

Not that I am drunk, on two mere glasses,
But I look forward to a time without meaning
When the only poem is the poem of pure description
Without transitive verbs, the verbs for action

Harrowing the landscape. John Deere tractors'
Mammoth tyretracks, dying into ice and hoarfrost
In the mud of farmyards, and the steel entrails
Of muckspreaders, freezing themselves

To an Iron Age of work and consciousness.
Evening deepens. Wait a while, stay out
In the winter sun, westering over black hedgerows,
Melting the lough into transcendental golds

Of whatever vintage—Chablis, Muscadet—
I am cold inside with. Chilled, subzero, white,
The crystallised world is giving up its essences
In ground-mist, in the blue of exhausts,

The steam off the flanks of animals, human breathings
Wreathed in condensation, and the decay
Of vapour-trails. A fuming of life into spirit—
Mountains cloud-hung, weightless. And the sound-world

Somewhere to the north, the flow of traffic
Ghosted in local fog, the twelve-bore pock
From the shooting-blinds, subliminally quietens,
Simultanaeous, at last, with its own echoes.

Binocular vision, stereoscopic mind
But just for an instant. Then the effect wears off.
Night, and the line of mercury will sink
To minus four, over ashes and hot whiskey,

The book of meanings. There, in its stand of pines,
A house awaits me. Bud, thorn and drop
Are cold beyond knowledge. And the inner ear,
Illiterate, rings with air like a glass.

ICY PANDEMONIUM

What the soul needs is silence and warmth. What it gets
is an icy pandemonium. —SIMONE WEIL

Snow on the Dublin mountains. Takeoff time—
  Through the wide glaze
Of departure lounges, runways rimed with ice,
Wings and tailfins spinning on a dime
For England, France. And it's goodbye, once again,
To the high stool at the counter, cigarette-haze,
To love made quietly, in a sacred room
Away from the family circle, the need to explain,

To the brief and glittering frenzy of Christmastide
  And the notion of home,
The ones who had children, the ones who were suicided,
The ones who made their distances in poems,
The silent siblings, still with something to prove
To me or themselves, the retroactive bore
Divided in himself since the Civil War,
The longplaying records, needles stuck in grooves,

The soul of discretion, the soul who can only scream,
  In short, to the weight of years
Come crashing silently down around my ears,
Though the city hang there, seemingly always the same,
Weaving, unweaving itself, in skeins of light
On the Liffey docklands, the cranes of the North Wall,
Carbides or magnesiums, day-for-night,
Brilliancies, on a depth of total recall. . . .

An hour and fifteen minutes flying time
    To Charles de Gaulle—
Who were the innocent? Who were the ones to blame?
Airborne, through the clouds, I hear it still,
The dialogue of the deaf, outshouting each other
In Nesbitt's or the Palace, rounds of drink
And souls come in from the cold, foregatherings,
The still, small voice, unable to hear itself think,

Salvaging, here and there, a living word
    From the drift of happenstance,
A soundbite or an anecdote, somebody met by chance,
The key to an inner mystery. Safe, *a bord*,
Between two worlds, suspended in mid-flight,
I dream of a bare table, the warmth to come,
A silence at the heart of Paris, a room,
Detached, anonymous, nothing to do but write.

I stop, because everything is happening here
On the Faubourg Saint-Denis
And somebody once, from another tradition,
Marked my cards. 'You will make your way through the world,
A man in a trance, sampling life like a long bazaar,
A marketplace of the senses . . .' And here they are
In the immigrant quarter—
African dates, and oranges in season
For it is deep winter, and the clothes-presses
Billowing steam, and the doors of hammams
Behind which bodies soak.

But what would he make of these, epiphany cakes
On sale by the baker's dozen,
Taking over Paris, in the days of undeclared Spring
And the blessing of baptismal waters?
Glazed, with an almond core of strangeness
And a paper crown, in memory of the Magi,
Those breakers with tradition.
I study one, to see what it is made of—
Epiphany: a brilliant showing-forth
Of the commonplace, in the instant of recognition—
And it falls apart in my hands.

And stooping down, through the Middle Eastern crowds,
I pick up an *objet trouvé.* Five centimes—
The lightest coin, of least denomination,

Numinous, free. A creature of marketplaces,
So they say, a martyr to the dropped word
In a foreign tongue, and the feast of associations—
No saint, but a go-between
On lines of faith and lost transcendence,
One who, in his time, has shamed the devil,
I was born for this, and other acts of retrieval.
It was said to me once, long ago.

THAUMATURGE

Not a day too soon, or too late,
   She entered his life
And left it behind her. Childless, taken to wife,
Anxious as a boy on his first blind date
Not to hold back now, in the danger zone
Of either/or, thronged with the skulls and crossbones
Of adulterers, and those gorgon stares,
Wronged women, at the tops of stairs

Beyond apology, he would never remember
   Time in the pleasure-chamber.
Naked, but for the mask of surgery
On a wounded physician, healer and thaumaturge,
She alone could slake his need to adore,
To trace the line of tibia and femur,
Penetrate, at last, to the liquid core
His life depended on, and sleep inside her

While her eyes stayed open. *Yes, I am shy of my breasts*
   But other than that—
Immaculate white skin, her belly flat,
A million husbands, into the mythic past,
Clandestine, brief. A widow cried next door
And the small hours deepened—*where on earth is this?*—
And suddenly in focus, on the floor,
Her own clean linen. No, she would not be kissed. . . .

All this from a jump-cut film, long ago—
    His terror in the hallway
Like them all. *Nobody else must know*
For both our sakes.... A moment, but for always...
Blandishments and masculine evasions,
Janus faces. Parked, three streets away,
Her company two-door, by an all-night station,
Luminous, blue. Tomorrow, through the in-tray

Filtering its faxes, strip cartoons
    Out of Mills and Boon
In two dimensions. One reversible call
From a public telephone. After that, the pall
Of work, years, ageing, and her ghostly fame
Spreading like a slander, through the daughters
Named for no-one, in the married quarters,
Family circles, as the children came.

Notebook Two

PARIS, AUGUST 1997–MARCH 1999

There it was, invisible electricity
In the kitchen, through an open window
Biding its time, as the halogen lamp
Smoked like a Roman cresset—dying insects!—
And the hot Provencal night, alive with treefrogs,
Crickets chirring, stirred the windowframe,
Rehearsing for an ultimate explosion,
Bringing the earth full circle.
                              'You were saying—'
The meal at the stage of wine-dregs, bread and olives,
Stones spat out the window. 'Well, I was saying
I grew in that same rottenness, humanity,
As Zola's L'Assommoir—a Paris tenement.
At the age of eight, I looked up from its pages
To the real thing, happening there on the bed.
My mother, you see, was dressmaker to the whores.
That was how they paid her—secondhand books.'

A cat at the end of the table, picking clean
The bones of a rabbit. Unwashed delph
On the draining-board, and the wooden latticework
Of a breadbin, high on the wall against rats.
'This, you know, was once the master bedroom
Centuries back. . . .' It seemed the keeper of wolves,
Primordial owner, slept through the degradation
Of his own house, deaf to the party-pieces
Dredged-up lines from Rimbaud's Bateau Ivre,

Rattled off, staccato, into the night,
The iced and yellow drams, the tinkling glasses,
Lemoncello. . . .
                    'Liqueur from Capri—
The *crème de la crème*. Capri itself is dead.'
Begonias, the trumpets of Jericho,
Blared in the dark. A splash from a swimming-pool,
Night-bathers, nude, in underwater lighting,
Playboys in the sway of a hunter's moon
And a lost age forming, old as Roman tesserae—
Storm or no storm, in a hundred years
Of idle chatter, stones spat out the window,
Someone, picking his way through heat and ruin,
Would start again in a plot of olive trees.

A big man, injury-prone
From local rugby, global war,
Dips his face in the living waters
Of L'Isle-sur-la-Sorgue.

Not once, but many times
Do we enter the same river,
Conjuring each other's names,
Feeling the old fever

Of the ancients under everything.
Abandoned on the riverbed,
The stone ear of a god
Appears to be listening

Beyond bridges, passing cars
And fighters screaming overhead,
To Heraclitus, René Char,
The pre-Socratic speech of the dead,

And that first, diluvian roar
Issuing, a few miles back,
From sheer Provencal rock.
Market day in L'Isle-sur-la-Sorgue—

A poet's sources . . . Way to the east
The silos, aimed at Anywhere,
Gravid with plutonium
And Heraclitean fire—

The rugby-mad, in seventh heaven,
Dancing on air. And the big man gone
Who wrote with an injured hand,
And the river shimmering on.

THE LITERAL VERSION

for Ranko Sladojevic

Behind it, I can just make out
The original. And further back
Something resembling a man—
For the name, even translated
To the language of the great world
Is masculine—

Shadowy though, forever snowbound
If the poems are much to go by,
A lone wolf, moping about
Unholy altitudes,
Borderline states. Unmarried,
Though a lover seems to visit

On Sundays at least, 'her lips'—
I am quoting from various texts—
'Ice-cold, pressed against my cheeks.'
And his weekends, snowed in
By a blizzard of football games
On changing screens, are given over

To cemetery visits, godlessness,
Bleak honesty. For the dead
Are everywhere—there has been war,
There will be again—
And irony, his one protector,
When it fails, leaves only silence,

A staring at walls, an autism.
Or the angel-dust
Of snow blown onto the floor
Through an open window—
Moments of grace.
The life lost in translation—

I barely approach it, even my own.
The rest is cyrillics,
Deaf institutes, homes for the blind.
A bridge is mentioned, more than once.
There is a sense of solitude
And a longing to connect.

Never having lived here, except in spirit
Or by proxy, through lovers and friends,
I'm tense for anyone's reappearance
As the doors cannon to, and the aftershocks sound
On the opposite houses. Blind at both ends,

Dark, with a sense of falling away,
I could never probably stand my ground,
Not now, in that state of mind
Where a woman of twenty-six, between boyfriends,
Laying out possessions, never intending to stay,

Takes out a lease, some five floors up from the street,
And the night-machinery, the lights
Of Dublin Port and Docks, the whiff of coal,
The shuntings at the railhead, tons of freight,
Drive their wedge of iron into her soul.

An hour has struck, for moral loneliness.
(May it never come back
After all this time . . .) A quartz clock
On the night-table, clothes in a gunny sack,
And sanctuary, for a while, from the middle classes—

One at work on a shooting-script, another painting tiles,
Another scraping cello-lessons, tiring after a while,
A woman with a baby on her own,
A man who broke down nightly, keeping a band on the road.
I limit myself to those I have known,

Who found themselves far out on the learning curve
For once in their lives,
Alternative; who changed, or lost their nerve,
And now are household names, or public men
Or vanished, and have never been heard of again,

Or may, for all I know, be living here
To this very day, through heightened windows
Eyeing me, for a rival or a peer,
A lover, who once slept over,
Returning to the unfinished business of years.

HEREAFTER

Perhaps only he who wants to finds eternity.

—EUGENIO MONTALE

They say, under certain conditions,
And maybe sleep is one of them,
The soul rises out of the body
And wanders about. And lying here
In the depths of the night, I hear him
Or his ghost, the old metronome
Of footfalls on the ceiling above me,
Unearthly stations, fiddled with,
Tuned into, or the sudden rush
Of cistern water, as an aged man
Relieves his prostate in the small hours.
They say his wife died long ago.
I was not here then. They say
There were children, or relatives,
So maybe it is one of them
Come back, days after the event,
To straighten things out. Or his own soul
Going about unfinished business
As ever, unopened correspondence
From his letterbox—collective memory,
The State, not letting him go just yet.
And the restaurant where he died,
The one at the corner, yet to be paid.
Two days after, wreaths on the landing,

Rumours. That is all I know—
The rest visions, reported sightings,
Local history. Man overboard
In the great sea of eternity
Where, maybe, he just potters about
As always, within earshot,
Thinly partitioned from the living,
Neither in heaven nor in hell,
Revisiting, under certain conditions—
Restless leg or alcohol in the veins—
Those of us without souls to lose
With news of the huge anti-climax.

You return, bewildered,
To a world where everyone is always young
And you alone have aged.

'Mass into energy, energy back into mass'
A student theorises to his girlfriend
Over Danish pastries, at a neighbouring table,

'And, of course, the question of time
And its reversal . . .'
                    Twenty
You would guess, the pair of them,

Like everyone else in the cyber-café,
Its blizzard of information
On-line, except for yourself the revenant

From the other side of the sky.
A slice off Newton's apple. Perfect knowledge.
Here they are eating it though, not watching it fall.

MONT SAINTE-GENEVIEVE

i.m. Séan Dunne, 1956–1995

If days, as they say, are one long abdication,
I into not-I, wearing away the mountain
Underfoot, then let it slide,
This complex of establishments, the shops
On the steep street downwards, the restaurants,
Ethnic, local, and the pubs,
The Russian bookstore, with its *émigré* texts,
The pretty, unapproachable women
Of the Latin Quarter, Sunday morning heat,
The *philosophes*, bohemian, effete,
The whole back catalogue of modern jazz
Like scree off an Irish hillside.
                                        Knockmealdowns
Or Commeraghs maybe. Either way
You are one of the ghostly now, inaudible feet
On an ageless treadmill. Better still,
Select, of the company of Marin-Marais,
Viola-da-gamba celebrant here, in another century,
Or Gabriel Marcel, who paused for thought,
It came to me on the Mont Sainte-Genevieve . . .
Driven, like yourself, by the need to believe.

The bottom of the hill, at Maubert metro—
The first mushrooms of autumn
In the Sunday market. A young Vietnamese

In her sunken tea-room, laying out white china,
Bowls and teapot, steaming green infusion
At the heart of a heat-raddled city—
The small thing done well.
                            One of your many stations,
Séan, the halfway house of accurate practice
Before the fullblown ritual over the river—
White, shrouded figures, members of the order
Of desert silence, at the heart of Paris,
Motionless, and your mind
Drifting in and out of the mysteries
To its own concerns, like our time together
Years ago, one winter evening in Cork,
Over glasses, in the silence of the Long Valley,
Half-full, half-empty. Then, as now,
No need for anything spoken. Only the mind
Worn down, like ancient stone,
By repetition, and monotony,
And the endless patter of the ego, fallen silent
At last, through suffering, through tiredness,
Through the plainchant of days
And the endless sway of chorus and antiphon.

Far into October, still blue and hot,
And the trees turning ash-coloured
And the acorns black on the floor of the royal forest,
Months ahead of themselves. A mushroom,
Penile, in the leafmould of years,
A blast of grouse from the underside of hedges
Into empty space. Notation—
The boar outruns its own mythology,
The king is dead, long live the king.
Desacralised, in a haze of unnatural weather,
Landscapes, unobserved sabbaths
Backlight the spires, that ring out only time
On a Sunday afternoon. Spent cartridges,
Gunfire. Hereabouts are hunters,
Spectral, in the extraordinary yellow
Of light and leafage. Faint terrestrial breeze.
The milky lines of flight-paths through the aether
Dissipating . . .
                    Write it on the hoof,
With the ages all conflated
And no regard for style. We are entering winter.

All rose, all became, in their own way,
Masters of the globe.
                And I watched them,
Human being that I was, outstripping me
By degrees, in field and classroom,
Grasping, so quickly, the calculus of change,
And later on, in great laboratories,
Stationary, all hand and eye
As the catalyst dripped in, and the colour changed
And the white magic of fume cupboards
Zoomed upwards—*poof!*—like a mushroom cloud.

Already, they had it over me.
Method. Accuracy. The suspension of feeling
For the matter in hand. Laughter was for afterwards,
Wisecracks, and the lines from Oscar Wilde
Who had an answer for everything.
The Eroica symphony—music while you work—
Played through a screen above us, raised the tone.
There were women—colleagues and assistants—
In starched white coats, already deckled
With the yellow of titrations,
Bright asbestos gloves and plastic goggles
Not concealing, for an instant, their femininity—
But that was for afterwards.
                Afterwards has arrived—
They have moved, the masters of institutes,

To the promised lands, and the countries of the future.
Cities are for touchdowns,
Conferences. God observes their sabbaths.
One of them dropped me a line the other day.
'I once saw Man as organs, now as enzymes. . . .'
Not, mind you, that I envied him,
I, with my jar of pens and my Olivetti,
Dealing, like an alchemist,
In concentrates, precipitates, and the retrograde heaven
Of my very own angel, nailed to the wall.

They had formed a republic,
A small one, in the depths of the forest,
The Belorussian forest. Partisans,
If you like, of a lost ideal—
Their uniform, if such it could be called,
A thing of rags and patches,
Battle fatigues, abandoned
In the advances, in the retreats
Of vast armies, passing away like phantoms.

Stillness. Dripping. Every sound
From the frightened chitter of birds
To the snap of a twig, invested with Greek meaning,
Hearkened to, preternaturally pure
In the presence of death
For inattention.
                    Herbs, and natural medicines—
To come back here, in lieu of family,
Hearth or village, since the very first winter
Blackened, razed. To stumble, one day,
By miracle, on the likeminded,
Pitching, striking camp,
Where women also fought, and men could cook,
And beauty was not forgotten.

By the third Spring, between the lines,
The rumbling grew much louder,

Switched direction. 'What century is it out there?'
Somebody read from Pasternak.
A new sadness, deeper than liberation,
Racked everyone. It would come, alright,
The future of mankind,
Bypassing them. For the time being,
The fight was elsewhere. Then, like a second thought,
Intelligence would smoke them out.
They would be handed over.

One by one, the secondhand images
Break away, and the ice-cap of the world
Starts drifting north, as if it could ever enter
This hemisphere of doubt and knowledge.

                                       Bergs
Nine-tenths below surface
Everyone has heard of, everyone seen
Emerging through the fifth wall of a television screen,
And the weird, submersible music
Of cetaceans—snorings, wails,
Their call-and-response, their electronic blips
A radio archive traps on acetate
And passes on. Their rapture of the deep.

And that is all I know about Antarctica—

Or nearly. For to describe the whaling station,
Human presence, in that trackless field,
Of sixty below zero, I can still call back
A wind-gauge, with its swirling cups,
A radio-mast, and the tedium of white nights
At anchor, slow butchery
And extraction, and the million barrels of oil—
Imagination on its austral flight
Above nothingness, gathering unto itself
The hunting grounds, the drink and cinema-huts,
The endless winter blizzards, till the mind cries *Cut!*—

And that is all I know about Antarctica.

It is cold, and getting colder. I am almost there
At the pole of pure unknowing.
The march is hard, but somehow satisfying.
Numbness and a wonderful fulfilment
Blend as one. The death-wish
You would say, when nothing is left
But the hammering of the heart against the head.
The whaling station, yapping dogs and sleds
Are nothing now. I have not moved an inch
Since the beginning of this long divestiture.
I will not be planting flags
Or laying claim to anything not my own.

THE ASTHMA VAN

For those of you with breathing difficulties
Remember the asthma van

As it made its rounds, on a Tuesday afternoon,
Trawling the estate, for girls and boys

Who couldn't keep up with the rest,
Whose cheeks turned blue, who pointed at their chests

And had to be taken away.
Internal claustrophobia—what did that mean?

In the language of allergens and histamines,
Albuterols and steroids, now, today,

If you felt it coming on, the airless state
Wherever you were, on a street, or a public platform,

They would have you on the ground in no time flat
As if the attack had been anticipated—

Gamma interferon, oxygen mask
Before you could even ask.

The fury of chronometers measuring time—
Just listen to them, ticking, ticking, ticking,
Cuckoo-blasts, alarms all over the shop
Where God the Watchmaker, alias the gnome
Who owns the place, is winding us both up
For nothing, handing our Tissots back
In synchronicity, loud as a beating heart
When held to the ear, beside a sleeping partner.

Step outside, now, into pure duration—
Dali's branches, dripping on the plain
Their liquid clockfaces. Walk, my love, don't run,
It makes no difference, where predestination
Bends the schedules. Yes, we will catch our train,
The first of hundreds, doing their mystical ton.

GRANDFATHER

i.m. William Brandon 1885–1945

This is the man to whom I owe my life—
And I never met him! Tearing off his clothes,
Quick, quick, on the Ypres salient, there he goes
In terror, from the threat of an almost-wife
Called Chlorine, Phosgene, Hydrocyanide,
Leaping the duckboards, past the slaughtered cows,
His handkerchief soaked in urine pressed to his nose—
Aboard a troopship home. I might have died....

Then Peace, the killing bottle, and the dropsy
Of the South Seas. Watch as he drowns in air
Like all the other shades, who were never spared
To take a native woman and grow older
In fake Paradise. Hear their shuffling steps
In the sightless realm, a hand on each others' shoulder.

SECULAR EDEN

Six o'clock in secular Eden—
No-one will ever fall from grace
Where the bells are electric, and the chimes
Of a French municipal hall
Preserve us in time.

The Place de la Grand Armée
Is empty. The Place de la Paix
With its locked-up church, and its one café,
Illuminates the flag of state
At the end of the Seventh Day.

A rattle of skateboards—
Children playing. There go lovers,
Crossing race and bloodline. And the flight-paths
Write their celestial Word
On the sky above us

In silence, on the deepening blue.
No guilt now, only vertigo
To the end of time, if anyone stops to think—
And the lights of cash-dispensers
From the all-night banks

Coming on, as if by a hidden hand.
And the *apokatastasis*
Of the healthfood shop, to be entered into,
With the pure, organic apple
There in its window.

And the last shall be first, and the first shall be last—
Herbivorous, nibbling at the runway's edge,
The rabbits quivering in our turbo-blast,
The lower forms, across the broken bridge

Of evolution, have us in their sights
And look beyond us, through the fuselage
Of a 747 trembling before flight,
A batman's signals, to their own Golden Age

Of wind and heavenly grass, already achieved.
Their race is over. Patiently they wait
As we lumber towards take-off, to receive us
At the infinite point where both our lines shall meet.

THE STONE

1

Late in life, attacks of the stone—
Galled, doubled over,
Travelling Europe all alone,
A wife and the ghosts of ancient lovers

Left behind in Aquitaine
For thermal springs and watering holes,
Who wouldn't know my name? Montaigne—
A body without a soul

Tracing its own arc
Through Augsburg, Baden, on to Rome
In agony, a falling star
From the sky beneath Saint Peter's dome,

A kidney patient, nothing more,
Discharging the slow gravel
Of inner breakdown, saddle-sore
As the track unravels.

Where the earth's fault
Opens, minerals bleed—
The irons, strontiums, Glauber salts
Your faithful servant needs.

2

It will outlive me,
The stone. It will never pass.
God may condemn me. God may forgive me,
But here where flesh is grass

And the laws of our condition
Comfortless, I will write a book,
The first without religion.
A manual of sex

For the beginner. Wise remarks
On raising children, bowel-evacuation,
How to stay sane in the dark.
A primer of earthly adaptation,

Me at the centre, average
In everything, especially pain—
Incurable by saxifrage,
Your mortal scribe Montaigne,

Who sees, through plague and slaughter,
The evil in God's plan,
Who keeps his dignity, son of man,
The trace of blood in his water.

A GULF STREAM ODE

i.m. Laura Allende 1907–1984

To the west of us, like an untold epic,
Huge and silent, written in air and water,
Nutrient salts, cold-walls and foggy banks
Dissolving in each other, threading their ways
Between the islands, Bofin, Inishturk
And the crooked nine-mile fjord of Killary Harbour,
Wittgenstein's cottage, Ownie King's post office,
Faherty's, around our summer house,
The Gulf Stream ran through childhood.
                                        High inland
I stopped a minute. For it was lifting,
The eternal mist, that blots out everything
To a distance of yards—a mist off the sea
I could conjure out of nowhere, to this very day,
Shrinking the world to microcosm. Waterdrops,
Fern-leaves. Squirming under my boot,
A hook in its gullet, the death-entanglements
Of a Sargasso eel. It was lifting,
And the distances, the space of pure imagining
Beyond the merely great-in-the-particular
Cleared like a depth of field. Away to the west
Were Carney's acres and his lazybeds,
Mullaghglass headland, with its burial-ground
Abutting on nothingness. Faraway no-sound—
Ocean breakers, cresting along their lengths.
And the rest a legend, as yet to be pieced together.

Yes indeed, we were an extraordinary family—
Granny Allende, our maternal ancestor,
Arucanian cheekbones, almost local,
With another life in London, summering here,
Our great enigma. How, I was asking myself
Even then, unfledged at twelve or thirteen—
How had we fetched up here, in this maritime state
Of 'warm wet winters, summers cool and damp'
Our house so filled with pebbles, sea-shells, bird-cries,
Hurricane-lamps, that threw gigantic shadows,
Calcified fishes, drifted tropical seeds
Inscrutable with oceanic force
The Gulf Stream brought us? Shadows, Granny Allende—
Even then, I was spooked by my own lost origins.
Not that it mattered here, if anywhere.
Wittgenstein, they said, was a very strange man.
And Slippey Faherty, with a hook for a hand,
Salting, smoking, curing in his shed
Horse-mackerel for the winter, cod and pollack.
Major Plaistow, back from Japanese camps,
Shacked up with a local girl. And Nora Burke
Abandoned by her man, on their wedding-night,
Who farmed the land alone.
                                        In my mind's eye
I could see her down there, swishing her great scythe
Through late July. I could see them all,
Inhabitants of the Gulf Stream, local, small,
Absorbed in their business. Ownie King
With his sheepdrops and his week-old telegrams,
Eavesdropping on Greenland and the late summer run,
The Irminger, the Humboldt, Norway currents,

Awaiting a poacher's moon. Again it would fall,
The north Atlantic mist, the long depression
Stretching to the Arctic. Blow-ins, storms,
Boreal darkness, night-time closing in.
I would deny everything. Whole decades would pass.

Meanwhile though, unkillable in the grass—
Granny Allende, where on earth did you come from?—
An eel was writhing. Instinct told me
Let the thing go. Coldblooded, let it melt
In its own element, an elver-memory,
Pure nacelle, of absolute Otherwhere,
Epic or legend, to get back to once again.

for Odile Hellier

As a place, to live and die and go mad in,
Chat up a stranger, seek out a clean apartment
Where cats, or even children, are allowed,
Where the heating is included, the ceilings rococo,
The landlords, whoever they are, forever absent,
The fourteenth district of Paris isn't the worst.
Beckett liked it—maybe he had no choice.
And Giacometti the sculptor set up shop
Around the corner—forty years in the same studio,
Pure as Diogenes.
                Those, of course, are the luminaries,
The exceptions. Vladimir Illyich Lenin,
God preserve his soul, out walking with Krupskaya,
One step ahead of the Tsarist secret police
In the Parc des Monsouris. And mad Louis Althusser,
The philosopher, in the Hopital Sainte-Anne,
Wondering what went wrong. The great and good
Who gave the streets their names, the overreachers
In every direction, id and superego—
Salvador Dali, Le General Leclerc—
Missing the obvious, going a stop too far.

But to get off here, with the ordinary mortals
Holding open doors for one another
At Denfert Rochereau, or the Place d'Alesia,

Dank underworlds, is to clear your head
In a secular air. The force of the city hits you—
Traffic a static blare, the clatter of feet
Through after-hours. And the post-religious shock
Of time forever stopped on the parish clock
Of Saint Pierre du Maine. The omni-tolerant nights,
The everydayness raised to a holy rite
At café tables. Ten francs, one for a tip—
For luck or superstition, who knows which,
Or the simple strengthening of the human bond
In a lonely hour, while some are being thrown out
And others sit there, in and out of season,
Dry-eyed, who stopped crying long ago
Over lost illusions.
                                    How it might have been,
How it might be yet, in the other nineteen districts,
Anyone may guess. A mile to the east
The Chinese quarter, west the electrified trains
Of Montparnasse. But in between,
A little left of centre, the quatorzieme,
All softness of acacia trees, and plane-trees,
Living off its pavements. Zeyer, Paris Orleans,
Blazing round the clock, like constellations
Where the lost-in-space drop in, the emigres getting by
On dubs and voices-over, scraps of translation,
Cadging kidney veal, a bone for the dog,
A taxi home. And the late-night florists
Georges and Georges, that happily married couple,
Making their own small corner in a world

Of outer darkness. If you died on your feet
An ambulance would arrive to pick you up
And guarantee your place in the universe.
True, it takes some luck and a little money
To set yourself up around here, but it can be done.

THE BATHHOUSE

It still exists, the bathhouse
Where the young Augustine washed himself,
But now it is everywhere

And the waters of the spirit
All steam, make wraiths out of men
In Paris, Constantinople,

Mosques and hammam dens
Wherever they are. The pummellings, the rubdowns,
Towelled bodies stretched on slabs,

And tea, in little glasses,
Green and sugared, sweetening the hour
Of deep, corporeal peace.

And to go on from there
Into sainthood, what would be required?
Don't tell me—supernatural fire

Beyond the melting-points
Of the corpulent, in their catechumenate
Of almost-souls,

Their boiling sauna cabinet.
Talking, gossiping, all might be the fathers
Of Augustine, to this very day

Observing, in their sons,
'The signs of active virility coming to life,'
Delighting in lines of likely descent

As the pre-baptismal waters
Rise around them—human, discredited even then
In the centuries of the body.

Imogen, straight as a die in a crooked world.
Just to look at you, soul-sister,
Threading your way through the maze of *Cymbeline,*
The ageless lies, the plots and counter-plots,
The blank verse speeches honouring chastity
Is to know slander.
                When the curtain rises
And you find yourself out there, already too late,
Exposure is total, everything unreal
Yet terrifying. The audience in the know
Is faceless, blank, too far beyond the footlights
And the close-up dazzle of events
You half-understand. The politics? Mere stagecraft.
Chastity? A word for your good name
In an age of cynics. Iachimo, Posthumous,
Cloten—deck them out in modern dress
And sell their stories off, to the yellow press.

Shamming dead in the cave of transformations
Hide yourself, then. '. . . *nor measure our good minds
By this rude place we live in. . . .*' Two bare rooms
For the down-and-out, the social reprobate,
As wild a place as any in that Britain
Before Christ. A typewriter, bearing witness,
Stammering out its vision of the truth
In widowhood. Forces, gathering

From abroad, beneath an alien caesar—
Earthly redemptions.

                      Yes, it will come again,
The hour of luck and personal vindication.
You will be loved in public for a while—
The hangman, temporarily frustrated
In the background, and the audience clapping,
Dematerialising, in its own abyss,
A whiff of smoke in your nostrils, from the auguries
Of the soothsayer, anxious as always to please.

Huge stanzas, on the end of the world,
Were crowding in like weather, scudding cloud
And changing light, on Monday the twenty-third
At the breakfast table. Light of heart
And casual, with the working week ahead,
We went to our rooms. Again, the traffic noise
Outside my window. Quieter, outside yours,
A garden, finches, at the back of the house.
And this we called our discipline, our art,
Internal, focussed, warding off the powers
Of dissolution, each in our own small way,
Ideal or real, sufficient unto the day.

As for myself, I was desperate to get back—
That sacred book, Augustine's *City of God*—
To a time behind our time, of plunder and sack,
Where the word Apocalypse was clearly stated.
Better not to write then, just to read—
To read and listen, only to bring in later
Everyday life, the baker up at four
Around the corner, six months from retirement
And his millionth loaf, the silence of mid-morning
On every floor, the boy delivering fliers,
The postgirl with her sad impetigoed face,
When the Beginning and End were definitely in place.

As for yourself, I hesitate to speak—
Doing it better than I, whatever you did—
With your pregnant myth, expanding by the hour,
Incorporating gardens into the Garden,
Burrowing into consciousness and id,
Abandoning Logos, cultivating Psyche,
Plot and character, what the butler saw
Of more than manners—in a word, real life,
For what did anyone know of Eternal Law?
Bypassing the Sublime for someone's grief,
Irrational, undignified, humanly true,
Staying faithful only to what you knew.

Eleven thirty. Carthage and Thagaste
Long since fallen, knew their gods had failed.
Alaric and his Huns had stove them in
Like Rome before them. Adeodatus the bastard
Of Augustine, and Augustine himself, were dead.
All that was left now was the *City of God*.
The orgies, the pomaded boys, the love-ins,
All were over. Outside, sirens wailed—
A truck rolled by, the windowglass vibrated.
Otherwise, all was normal. In your room
Another sentence formed. *For even without him*
Her life would go on. I stood in the kitchen, waited

For coffee to boil, and time to come to an end.
Monday, the day for maids. Behind the garden
Whiteclad women put their house in order.
One, who had just stayed over, ran her hands

Along her cheekbones, loving herself in a mirror,
Rubbing facecream in. A morning after—
Sinless, without guilt. Supernatural terror?
I could hear her hard, ironical laughter
Echoing through the ages, the sacked empires,
Back to Alaric. No, on the twenty-third,
For all its cloud-apocalypse funeral pyres,
Women, it seemed, would have the final word.

Notebook Three

PARIS–DUBLIN–PARIS,
APRIL 1999–DECEMBER 1999

THE PLACE

Unnameable, that blinding sheet of water
High in the hills I came upon out of the blue
And off the map, on my own way through
The sites of famine and the sites of slaughter

That called themselves Ireland. I had fished it, of course,
In childhood. That much, at least, was clear—
How deep it was, how wadeable its shores
The Ice Age left behind, how black and sheer

Whenever I saw beyond my own reflection
To an absolute depth. There was nothing there
But the myth of the arctic char, and water-boatmen,
Immortal, in their diving-bells of air.

And I remembered Michael, Desmond, Charles,
And Harry Cooling, crowding down like cattle
In their huge enthusiasm, to the water's edge—
All of them anglers, now, in the lake of darkness

Where the fence gives up its ghost, and the drystone wall,
At six-foot depth. *Show me the black points*
On your X-ray plate, I'll show you a race of giants,
Prelapsarian, thriving before the Fall.

I was pushing an open gate. Its rusty scrake
Was a raven's caw blown off the neighbouring peaks.
How lonely it might be, to swim there naked,
I could only imagine. Ireland, so to speak,

Had come between us, like a foreign word.
I saw right through it, in a state of grace
And absolute certainty, with the shadow-world
Of travel behind me. This, at last, was the place.

In she comes, through the swingdoor
Of a French café, like a brilliant emanation
Off the winter streets
To take the one available seat.

And she lights up
Instantly. Le Monde and a coffee-cup
Appear beside her. Unseeing
She reads, or she appears to read,
And her spoon steams, and Paris itself disappears
In that marvellous fug
Surrounding her, like an atmosphere.

It is one of those days
Of wintry light, transfiguring everything
Like a nimbus. Her hand strays,
With the whole place watching, up to her hair—
A page turns, in the history of being,
Unconscious, but aware.

LÓDŹ

for Ewa Chrusciel

Between thumb and forefinger
A city crumbles. I love it, though,
For all that rubs off, the living dust
Of people and situations,

The life, like a grainy film,
Black and white, turned technicolour
Flecked with post-industrial grime—
My own lost childhood, stopped in time.

Lódź, pronounced *wudge*.
To the foreigner, who always comes
As executioner-judge
From the West, or the East,

The women will all seem innocent
Of their own beauty, and the open pits
Beyond the city limits
Guilt by association.

A blind man, with a long white stick,
Enters his own courtyard
By sheer feel. Am I dreaming
Or did they never happen,

The Nineteen-Fifties,
Until now? A tram clangs,
And the passengers, time-travellers,
Waft through another twentieth century

Where everything is instinctive,
Where the id is still unheard of
And the churches overflow
On the Sunday pavements,

Where the age of perfect dentistry
Has yet to bare its teeth,
And the man I was meant to be
Must not be seen talking to me.

THE BALL

I was born to walk in the middle ground
And here it is, this fine May morning
Flanked with sycamores, where the lane curves round

And a half-world emerges,
The half-world of religious contemplation,
Darkened continents, swallowed words and urges,

Fallow convent land.
There, they live by silence
It is said, and nothing is ever owned,

And no-one is visible,
When well we ever get there,
Mother and I? Already, it seems impossible

We can ever go home.
The lowings, buckets, milk and cheese,
The Charollais herds—and a novice, in her own time,

Doing yard-work, like a kind of prayer.
A face turned away from the world
Is waiting for us, on the other side of the air,

But all I can see is close-up green, the tracery
Of creation, in a fat May leaf.
Again, it will be given to me,

The ball, for I have been here before
And watched it come around
Like a miracle through the wall, on its blind swingdoor,

A gift from an inner sanctum.
Mother will whisper. Someone will reply
In a hidden voice. It is God, of course, I must thank

For giving it back to me, lost and found,
From the dark side of the moon,
To bounce and bounce, on the unshatterable ground.

FREEZE FRAME

Climbing over a stile, or crossing a field,
Even as I see him, that man is freezing in time,

My father, and God is collecting the gesture
Or call it a statue now, which we all walk around

For there is nothing more to add. It happened,
I was there. Without knowing it

I was in at the death, and the frozen moment
Flows right through me, cold, electric,

Ever to be present. Is it memory
Or the Last Judgement? Time will never tell.

THE OTHER SHORE

I shout, but there is no echo,
Let alone an answer.

Father, are you listening over there
On the other shore?

If you hear me, start moving
So we can meet,

And the miles of blanket bog between us
And the dark water,

The wind, that makes a no-sound
Of my cupped hands,

Will cancel themselves out.
Time is passing,

Distance does not diminish,
Yet I could swear

I see you, far away over there
On the other shore,

Waist-deep in your depthless element,
Unconcerned, casting.

For you, all time has stopped,
That much is clear,

But here, it grows ever colder,
And the driftwood of an eternal autumn

Keeps coming in, on every wave.
I blow the foam off hollowed-out reeds,

I build a fire of stones and sedges,
Lonely for an answer.

THE ELDEST SON

The eldest son sees deepest into the past,
Forever looking backwards, over the shoulders

Of a generation carrying him, on a corridor
Dark and endless, smelling of food and medicine,

Human ordure, with the rooms thrown open—
Hospital, Home. A woman in there at her stove

Is soundlessly weeping. Bevies of aunts and uncles,
Next one down, are sharing an ancient secret—

Shut that bloody door! A brother and sister,
Nakedly playing, before the Age of Reason,

Freeze in horror, guilty of being seen.
And all the unmentionables, the remittance men

From the ends of the earth, the family ghosts
In winding-sheets, take up their beds and walk,

Forever being born, towards redemption.
All the doors are closing, one by one,

And baptism waits, the cruets, water, oil,
The change of state. As if he still might live,

The eldest son, the last to be brought down,
With the others long since gone into the future

And the afterbirth mopped up, the blood and tears,
The delivery ward by now a mausoleum.

THE STREET OF THE FOUR WINDS

After the liquid lunches, the slippage and lost ground
Of so many cities, and trying to find our feet
On alien pavements, your lore and my lore,
Let's have another, and where do we go from here,
That well-known little-spoken-of discreet
Establishment on the Street of the Four Winds,

Open all day and night, its empty afternoons
For rent by the hour, will take us in,
No questions asked, the ghosts of others' honeymoons
Who have left their overnight bags and gone on the town.
And there the state of marriage and living in sin,
The one in the other, the bed of straw and the bed of down,

Will be given us to make love in, and doze
Till the chime of awakening, and the chambermaid's knock.
And whose are they anyway, these borrowed keys
To our own pure strangeness, on somebody else's sheets?
Whatever you do, don't go to the window and look
Or ask which year, which city. Four Winds Street—

An indigence, a dream of dining out
On the goodwill of millions, as they go about
Unconscious business, here or anywhere,
Letting us be. Above, the hangman's rope
Of a naked lightbulb, as you pin your hair.
A Gideon bible to swear by, and a cake of fragrant soap

Like a *vade mecum*, to be pocketed free and taken
Into the latening world, of goings-home,
Old marriages. Again they will come,
The honeymoon couples, full of all they have seen,
To look right through us, like a might-have-been
Or another life, in a room they have mistaken.

RED FOX COUNTRY

I watched myself disappear
Off the bookshelves, and went away
To live them through, the invisible years.
And that is where I am today,

In red fox country, forking left
Beyond Armagh, around Lough Neagh
And through to Toome, the back way.
Spirit, intellect or gift—

For now, they have had their day,
And it calms me, this limbo
Where all, like myself, devoid of Grace
In a wilderness of symbols,

Must wait for the lights to change.
Salvation say the walls.
And I, whose numberplates are strange,
Whose accent anyone can tell

For a lost soul, a broken heart
From the Free and Fallen State,
Must colonise my own backyard
With the hour latening,

And the fox, the interloper,
A redgold streak, running deeper
In his own country. Sam Brown belts,
A word at the window. Pelts

Of hedgehog, badger, stoat,
The terrible rictus of the slain
On the straight and narrow. Wave me on
To a life beyond Dungannon,

A life beyond Cookstown, Moneymore,
Where true redemption starts.
A human house. A wind off the Shore.
And a woman from these parts

—*Deirdre, Deirdre, sandman's daughter,*
Tonight let us lie, like oil on water—
Sheltering me, with a broken gamp
And the yolk of a hurricane-lamp

As I fall asleep at the wheel
With red fox country all around,
Ever less visible, ever more real,
Running myself to ground.

That maddened, maddening blare
In India, near Lucknow,
A hundred years ago,
Trumpeting its terror,

Trailing its own afterbirth
Through villages and chain-gangs,
Flaring ears as wide as wings,
And the flattened hearths

Where something had gone through them
Like a natural force,
And somebody taking aim,
An ancestor, of course,

With all that lifeblood cornered, mute,
And the species dying
Already, and the orphaned young—
And afterwards, the foot,

All that remains, to this very day,
Sawn-off and silver-plated,
Starting its long migration
Through history, through hearsay,

Empire break-up, orange, green,
Through trampled genes
And shattered nerves, to the mantelpiece
Of a family on its knees.

THE BIRD-HAUNT

They had changed their throats and had the throats of birds.

—W. B. YEATS

Soon enough, they will come to me,
The birds, as I hunker here
In a wooden blind, on the shores of Lough Neagh,
Alone and cold, but never lonely.
All the souls will come to me,

Their given names changed
To Mallard, Moorhen, Mandarin, Merganser,
Chooking in among the reeds
Or a blatter of wings on the water
Of an absolute take-off.

Half the world has gone south—
It's winter now.... Self-insulated,
Deathless, last of the early Irish hermits,
I lift the hatch like a desktop
And light floods in,

A giant scriptorium,
Sky and water. Antrim to the east,
Its reef of lights. And the dot–dash–dot
Of a pollan-fleet, on the far horizon.
And the planes, the trajectories,

Flickering endlessly in and out
Of Aldergrove airport.
An hour from now, it will be dark
And arctic. November—
The month of the long south-westerlies

And conning the lists of the dead.
Brent Goose, Whooper,
Seagull, Diver, even a notional Grebe,
Their high, piping cries
Barely audible

In the uproar of the world.
On a carpet of blackened leaves
I blew in here. And now, suspended,
My mind amphibious
Between two elements,

With the dry cough of the wildfowlers' guns
In my ears, they return to me,
Desmond, Johnny, Michael, Margaret, Charles—
Crossed over, gone but still watched for,
Dark against the water.

Notebook Four

PARIS–SYDNEY–PARIS,
JANUARY 2000–DECEMBER 2002

THE CURE FOR COLOURBLINDNESS

Madonna of the Orange Tree, Conegliano 1459–1517

Eyesight given up on, rod and cone cells
Blown like bulbs, incipient darkness
Brings me now to the garden I can see clearly into,

Still as a picture, windless and complete,
Where the primary images hover.
Donkey, Virgin Mother, old Saint Joseph

Fostering a divinity that yells and kicks its legs
And stares off into the Infinite.
Pause, on the flight to Egypt. Wet-nurse duty,

Dockleaves for the ass, a rock to rest on.
Here, I enter the picture
After the lifelong trial of the eyes,

Now, in second childhood. Mother a Virgo
And her lovely substitutes
Hanging above me, oranges in bloom,

Father an old Saint Joseph, only there
In foster-care of the soul.
To be still going, already arrived,

Forever out of season, is heaven on earth.
A bird pecks in the foreground
And the avoided cities, where innocence was slaughtered,

Hang in the distance. Grace, protection,
Sheer haphazard, as you will,
Bring me now by galleries, flights of stairs,

Whole Venices, to the presence of a garden
Where the artist signs off
And the rest is death, or the cure for colourblindness.

ANTICHRIST

... daughter of night and times gone by —ALEXANDER BLOK

The snow falls, in that country—
Call it Poland. And the leaves
Like anywhere. As for the century
Let it be anyone's guess—
The old idea of good and evil,
The man-god not yet come to pass,

The insurrections, high ideals,
The exiles blown to the four winds,
The meat-and-potato meals
And the failure gone to ground,
The drunkards of Franz Jozsef Park
In an old provincial dark,

And leaning forward, the same girl
As always, after midnight,
With a gentleman from the world
'Who shares with us, tonight, his Writing'
Out of Paris, Moscow, stars
At the empty heart of the universe.

Their old Copernican globe,
Their white Mazovian linen,
Guild and tavern, market-stalls—
In half an hour, he has seen it all,
When the uncontaminated women
In the half-filled hall

Have scattered, there is only her
In the single bar left open
Now, along Cloth Merchant Square,
And nothing is going to happen.
Sabbatical starch and borrowed fur,
Her voice, her feminine air

Eternally out of date
But fetching, and her twenty years
That gather to a silent scream
'For Christ's sake, get me out of here!'
Her letters to the great
Unanswered, and the ghastly poems

Of her young, consumptive friends—
May the wages of oblivion
Pay them all!—are ashes in the wind
Of a pleasure-past where everything goes.
Lechery. Vanity. Sins, forgivable
But for the hairs in his nose,

His snuffbox, onion-flavoured breath
And the age about to close.
Outside, it is winter, silence, death,
Anus Mundi, the fate of the Jews,
Are small-talk, names to conjure with.
And tomorrow, he knows,

She will be there at the station,
Rain, hail or snow,
To see him off, in the long ago
Of the Life to Come, traditional,
With vodka spiked on bison grass
And a sign of the cross.

Matchbox sculptures, little poems—
Is that what you do with your life?

Everywhere, people in panic,
Fleeing. Paris, the open city,

Undefended, is every city,
Switzerland every refuge.

Every train is the only train
Still running, to the hoped-for land,

And millions, in flight from themselves,
Are dying to get aboard.

But you, you stand there
Mesmerised. An hour ago

A naked woman, in a strange hotel,
Made love to, and failed

At the point of ecstasy—
When will you ever see her again?

'It is the principle involved—
Truth, Beauty,

Call it what you will,
Belittle it ...' Travelling light,

Your lifework, inch-high sculpture
Crammed in a matchbox

Weighs nothing, in the scale of things.
All who can go have long since gone,

And soon the stations will empty.
In the breathing-space

Between ages, with the city deserted,
Eerily quiet, everything lost,

Already, she comes back to you
Out of an infinite distance,

Naked, mythical, one inch high
On the other side of time.

THE WRITERS BUILDING

The apartment's dumb as paper —OSIP MANDELSTAM

Writers building, writers block.
'I watched those lazy bourgeois swine
For twenty minutes by the clock—
Not one of them has written a line!'

A corridor in Iowa City,
Soundless, endless. Iron doors,
And the servants of Truth and Beauty
Whispering through them. 'Was there a war?

I don't remember, maybe you do. . . .'
'Here in the Midwest,
There is no more future, no more past.'
A scream, a suicide or two,

An Apple Mac hurled into the lake,
But generally, time to think,
To feel the mind go quietly blank
As the absolutes take—

Missouri silos, missile sites,
The snow, the old ballistic night,
Wet highways, an American dream
Where endlessly, the headlights stream

And all the windows run together,
Meltdown-vision, double-glaze
And suspiration, lonely breathers,
Lonely fingertips that trace

Their own self-image on the glass.
'Warhol did a portrait
Of our sponsor, you know—that magnate
From Des Moines.' 'The time will pass—

It always does. For now, I've bought
A ten-gallon hat, eat steak
For breakfast, and wear rhinestone boots—
But Real Life will come back. . . .'

Door twenty-five. Door thirty-two.
'I'm giving it back, Mohammedan spy—
I killed it for you, your fly!'
The many who were once the few,

The dream of higher consciousness,
The heat, the light, the rooms with a view,
The rush of air as a windowglass
Blew out, and the vacuum grew.

India now. And Spring, on the face of the earth,
Was changing into autumn. . . . Summer, far below
And out of reach, had blanketed Lucknow
In heat and darkness. Latitude fifteen north—
De Chardin's *The Phenomenon of Man*
For in-flight reading. Cities, thinking mass,
The spattered lymph of earthlight, stadium-glow
In the Himalayas. Blissed-out, fanned,
Their cabin-pressure flipped to laughing-gas,
The plugged-in to the endless movie-show

Were barely sentient. I was older now
By twenty years. She was down there, dead or sleeping,
Deep in an Asian city's sweetened soi—
High up there, on the inside of your thigh,
Do you wear me still, like a love-bite or a scar,
A token from the end of the Cold War
Between men and women? Summer far below
And out of reach. . . . I had left it in her keeping,
Gone with De Chardin and his triple vow,
Obedience, chastity, poverty, getting high

On rediscovered bones and burial sites,
The Irriwaddy, Indus, Mekong basins,
Australopithecus and Java Man—
Père Teilhard, digging deep between the wars
For higher reason. Soon it would be light

On Indochina, Bangkok, Singapore,
A million sparks of human consciousness
Slowly coming awake. And us up here
At the hour of breakfast, of the light collation,
Dwindling into spirit, in the cool noosphere,

De Chardin's element, pure perfectible mind.
The Movie Marathon—could I Go the Distance?
Eight hours yet. *Who knows, have I left you behind*
Or taken you with me, muse and dark ladie?
Masks of reassurance, stewardesses
Moved among us, shadowy, insistent,
Gathering from the drunks their half-filled glasses,
Calling time. Insomniac, afraid,
Remembering her, a second self betrayed,
A life passed over . . . Still, I had work in hand,

A place to get to. Once again The End
On the endless screen. De Chardin's point omega—
Sydney Australia. There I would descend
As purified as Christ or Martin Eden
From a night of reading. Humanly divine
As Teilhard wrote. And feeling my own lost Spring
Fast-forward into autumn. Screeches, mocking cries,
The too-late-now of nightfall cockatoos,
The laughter of kookaburras, currawongs,
Pacific time and weather, the end of the line.

At Darlinghurst, the ghost of Kenneth Slessor,
Last of the poets, in a bright bow tie,
Elizabethan, heterosexual, dated,
Came alive through the neon of King's Cross,
Australia's one bohemia, its density
Of good and evil, concentratedness,
Its scapegoats and its famous ways to die.

Drinkers of raw spirits, women on methadone
In secular chapels where the failed atone
For wholesomeness up-country; mirror-balls
Of strip-joints, and the rain on William Street,
The ruined innocence of the American Seventh Fleet—
And there he was, the author of *Five Bells*,

A little dandified, a latter-day Heine
With the City behind him, and the darkling lights
Of Sydney harbour, as the ferries plied
From Wilson's Point, Rushcutters and Balmain,
An intercutting bilge-wash, spectral white,
Of death and engines. Not that he ever died,

That spectre 'groaning to God from Darlinghurst',
Far from health and innocence, lost to the Good Fight.
Wilderness or City—which came first?
Ten thousand miles from home, in the drizzling night's
Pacific winter city foghorn drone,
I slept with the damned, a little less alone.

SYDNEY AWNINGS

There was no great heat, but the people were all out,
Basking, you might say, at the end of the world,

In the shadow of great awnings, sidewalk cafeterias,
Botany Bay, Victoria, Bondi Beach,

The glittering sea to the east, then nothingness,
Then New Zealand. *Send them back where they came from!*

Warnie does it again for Australia.
Newspapers, rustling. And a loveliness of legs

Extended under tables. Books laid aside
To look the sun in the eye, just once without blinking,

Drink up Eden, see the Pacific and die.
Nowhere, not up-country, its cattle and flies,

The ten-gallon headgear of its cricket fields,
Or the great north reef, wore hats with so broad a brim

As a Sydney awning. Nowhere so vast a shadow
Kept the people back from their final selves,

The laidback, absolute Saturday afternoon
Of shattered myth, lost chains, emancipation.

VICTROLA MUSIC

Hart Crane 1899–1932

Wind the damned thing up,
Release the handle, and begin your dance
For the millionth time. When it stops
And a crowd has gathered, start all over again.
From the front to the back of your brain,
Something is moving—a trance,

The cranked-up ecstasy
Of latter days. You are getting there—
Ignore them, those with no morrow
Or jobs, at the heart of despair,
Their ears stuffed with cotton wadding,
Who climbed out of the body

Only yesterday. Silent shouts
Mean nothing. But the automatic language
Shuddering through you now,
The news from nowhere, feel it spew
White paper, writing itself out
Like a telex message

On the left side of your mind.
King Oliver, Cannonball Adderley, Earl Hines—
Just keep them turning! The nightsoil man
From Attica, the Brooklyn Irish cop
Summoned by switchboard, to get you to stop,
Are pounding their own jungle beat

If only they knew it,
If only they could get through to it—
One more time! The dawn is breaking
On Sand Street, the sailors are all going home
To bottomless oceans. Seventy Eights
And the makings of a poem—

Gather them up, like dinner-plates
Indigence dines off. Soul-food
No-one ever ate or went to work on.
Mindblowing spirit hash, and residue
Of the devil's music. Which, anyway, means God
For the likes of you.

CAUL

I was wrapped in mine
On arrival, and it hit me,
The orange undersea light
Of the day of birth.

I was safe, though,
Unafraid of drowning
In the strange, new element
I had dropped into,

A man in a bathyscape
Of throwaway skin,
Old veins, post-natal,
Making his way in the world.

Some spoke of greatness,
Others of safety at sea.
Of the lying-in ward
Three pillars remain

And a great emotion.
Mother, am I beloved,
Or who else wears it now,
My dried skin cap,

For luck, on another ocean?

FACING MECCA

When the cook downed tools,
We all knew something was happening.
For menu, the dietary rules
Of Islam. Each evening

Silence, prayer, a thumbed Koran
And the whole place gone to hell
For the length of Ramadan.
Through the plate-glass window

A city in passing, amazed,
Looked in at the empty dining-room,
The mat on the floor, and the brass
Of an age-old compass—

Needle and orientation,
Pure belief. Now kneeling,
Now prostrate, as the psalmody
Dictated, orderly, calm,

He was facing Mecca.
Ley-lines, false meridians
Meant nothing. He was getting there
On the steam of a travelling-kettle,

Where pilgrimage, like prayer,
Is to the centre of one's whole being.
We watched him, all November
In the darkened city, unseeing,

As the rain beat down outside
And business died.
Instinctively, he would know
When everything came to an end.

We would hear him, through the long sleep
Of infidelity, slaughtering sheep
Made perfect by the law
In our courtyards below.

Old, old country ... No-one goes too far
  In the space of a life.
Me neither, driving. Where I took to wife
I will some day die—and the juggernauts, the cars
Ahead of me in the rain, or coming up fast
On the outer lane, are all going west
In both directions. I never did buy, I rent—
And the mileages, the clapped-out leatherette,
The whiff of sex and scorch-marked cigarette,
Are someone else's. Everything is lent
Or traded in around here for something better,
Contracts sealed in spirit, not in letter.

That's Hamilton's on the right. A sold franchise—
  Motorway bacon and eggs,
Adrenalin, petrol, sweets, the tabloid news.
A son looks after the paperwork. Breasts and legs,
Pirelli calendars. Outside, the rusty fleet
I borrow from. White, of course, is disaster,
Injury-prone, a gift to the panel-beater.
Sandra, the daughter, manages the kitchens.
Two hired women, one of each religion,
Break bread in silence, under a Safety poster,
Radio blaring, husbands on parole.
To think that she and the wife were once at school. . . .

And where I fit, in the general scheme of things,
    The loyalties, bad debts
Before my time, the bottomless rights and wrongs,
Is anyone's guess. Indefinite, indeterminate,
Ghosting the motorway's blown ionosphere—
Tail-lights, spray and droplets of exhaust
That crawl on the windscreen, sluice themselves away
On the blind arm of a wiper. Women's tears—
The infinite flat country under the mist
That drinks itself forever. Make my day
And take the slip-road, Mister. Clear my sight
For darkness at broad noon, the oncoming lights,

And the junkyard coming up now, on the right,
    That marks my exit.
Hamilton's portakabin, raised on bricks,
Where gypsies once pitched camp—old fly-by-nights,
Their tinsmiths' fires, their trade in stolen goods
A vanished chapter. Mine not to ask why.
The rainbow-coloured seepages, bad blood
Off rusted axle, bodywork and hub
Are in-laws trucks. The sleeping dogs let lie
Are toothless now. The beautiful bodies stripped,
Disintegrate, where everything ends up,
In the gene-pool, oily black, a thousand years deep,

Of Hamilton's stolen ground. I owe him keys,
    A car, the bride-price
Of my wife, and the house she half-inherits
In the dark trees, her terror of white spirits,

Ravaged innocence. Everything given back
Is one day closer to the breaker's yard—
Old Roadrunner Leyland Goodyear Bridgestone Ford,
Old concertina'd metal, pulverised,
Old blow-outs, tyres. Old country, going black
With original sin. Who marries into it, dies.
The man who wed us wore a Roman collar,
Hamilton sealed our vows, with a silver dollar.

They are his mountains, the Air Mountains,
And they hang there, in childhood
And old age, and everything in between
Is a mirage, though he does not know it—
The *wadi* where he grows, the chequerboard of green

That is high Numidia. Bishops and proconsuls
Sitting on squares like chessmen
In an immemorial game. The grafted olive takes
And bleeds clear oil, and the night,
Its superstitious shadows vanquished by reading-light,

Wakes to a dawn of advancement, in the knowledge-factory
Of Carthage. Where a door opens,
Coin is taken, and a hermaphrodite
Shows him upstairs, to the lewd Mithraic rites
On the mezzanine. Two hired women, seven men,

Kicking each other away, on the filthy sheets,
An octogenarian watching.
Darkness, but for a shaft of dusty light
Above in the roofbeams.
Lux interiora, he has taught himself to call it

All those decades later, when Rome itself is no more
And Carthage a weed-grown think-tank
For the defeated, in the lee of Punic Wars.
Lux interiora, light from within.
Desolate middle age, and the strength to begin—

To stumble down the stony watercourse
To Bizerta, a shadow in black robes
Among the landowners, their aloes, corn and slaves,
Their amulets against the Evil Eye,
Their *lares*, household gods, instinctual drives,
Their horses cannoning loose, and their crazes to die.

Foreshortened, the years crowd up to him like horizons.
Childhood again is near.
The sea, imagined once in a glass of water,
Again grows small. Concubinage, war
And orphaned knowledge, are no-roads to the interior.

There is snow on the Air Mountains. He is going there
To be cold in the Sahara
So far south, and know an impossible climate—
Hoggar, Atlas, Mountains of the Moon
Hanging outside gravity, before and after time.

To be spoken of in the same breath
Endlessly—Dunbar, Henryson,
Rivals maybe, poets both,
Two stone cottages knocked into one,

Two bachelors, a space between
The length of a generation
Or the trackless miles from Dunfermline
To Saint Andrews, the Scottish nation

A fifteenth-century mist
Where reputations, fate-lines blur,
And the battles lost
Are Flodden and time. The smoke clears

From the culverins. Dunbar staggers away,
His obsolete *Thistle and Rose*
Tucked beneath clerical clothes,
While Henryson, at the end of his days,

Rhymes *oaken board* with *hard turd*
And passes on of the flux.
No known descendants, only words—
Demotic, aureate. Rip-offs, texts,

The *Cresseid* and *The Bludy Serk*,
Two Married Women and the Widow,
The rest a vanishing into dark,
An afterlife in each others' shadow.

Sometimes, I look over the garden wall
And see her in there, working.
Far gone, in the good sense, she stoops
Among blind plants, and the vegetables
That give of themselves, this late in the year.
Weeding, hoeing, in an old coat,
October round the corner, bracing herself
On great legs, dragging at something invisible
From this distance, anyway.
The yellow snake of an ancient hosepipe
Curls on the dirtpath. Buckets of old rainwater,
August leftovers, brim and grow rusty
Among windfalls. But the air is still,
And the dimension she inhabits
Inaccessible. To get to her there
I would have to gatecrash time as well as space,
So far ahead of me is she now
In years, in knowledge. Not old though,
Not just yet. Still in her full strength.
I see no children, ever.
Sometimes a man. Onions, radishes, carrots,
Anything with a root, and the gnarled old fruit-trees,
The carnations, the blue cornflowers—
Not for the market though, or the flower-stalls
Of Lily of the Valley, unimaginable
Firsts of May, the feast-days of human labour.
No, she is doing it only for herself,

In her realm of sackcloth and ashes. I would join her there,
If time and the world allowed,
Burning the old grasses, threading the new tendrils,
Binding the shoots, and bringing bread
To the altar of a bird-table lodged in a tree-fork.
Starlings, bluetits, chaffinches, a wren—
And the blackbird chittering louder in the new bareness,
The clarified air. And leaf-smell, herb-smell,
Imperceptible earth. Again, she stoops
Inside the mystery, reaches for something,
Finds it. Blind to me,
Mindful, a soul feeding itself
On green minutiae, secretly in league
With the excluded, her spectacles catch the light
Unseeingly, as I lean there
Deep in September, fleetingly present,
Not asked in, though something is always given.

DOCTOR BENN

Gottfried Benn 1886–1956

Practitioners in poor neighbourhoods
Everywhere, in the aftermaths of wars
And reputations, Doctor Benn,
Physician and poet, soldier and survivor,
Is open for consultation.

It is not you, he says, who are sick.
It is the age, inside you,
That is sick. Your waiting-rooms
And patients, grains of insulin, morphine,
Are all beside the point.

Professional ethics bore you.
You would love him, just once, to talk about Poetry.
He smiles, politely,
Changes the subject. 'That garden'
He says 'You see it? On the plot of wasteland

Between ruins, its smoke-drift of autumn,
Compost fires, potato drills in leaf—
The woman who tends it, far gone in years,
Her gabardine belted with old rope,
Her headscarf, veteran's scars,
Is everything to me. . . .'

Sometimes he helps her, smoking a cigar.
No one reads him now, of course.
He would sleep, he says, through whole bombardments,
Believing in nothing anymore—
Untouchable, pure.

THE WEEPING STONE

Later, lost among half-tones,
Aftermaths, shattered lives,
The loverless daughters, sons without wives,
The self-hung and the drowned,
You may seek it out, the weeping stone
On which this house is founded.

It is down there, under everything,
Where the elements join—
Water, stone. The blistered wall,
The ripped-up floor, old weatherings,
Have their own tale to tell.
But to draw off pain,

To be shaken but indestructible,
Where are the ancient ducts?
Get down, now, on your hands and knees
Among murderous daughters,
Dumbstruck sons who hold their peace,
And feel for water

Where it enters stone.
Everything, the furniture, books,
The table where you eat alone,
Has a drained look.
Blameless, simply the last
To feel for the past,

You may ask yourself, in your empty house,
How it swallowed oceans
All those years, how the laws
Of water and stone are dry-eyed, emotionless.
You may find it, in the name of truth,
And prise it out like a tooth.

THE BLACK DOOR

Any day now, she will rise
And re-enter it, the black door
At the end of the yard,
And vanish forever.

Meanwhile, in the window,
Life is all foreground.
Nearnesses bloom,
The here, the now,

In the clays and manures
Of everyday. Midden-heap,
Compost, chicken-feed and flower
Monopolise the hour,

While something tries to come through—
Child-cries, weather, illusion—
From the middle distance
Clearing, over fifty years,

And closing up again.
But the door is always open,
The black door, unhinged,
Unhingeing, where the swallows flit,

Little Persephones
Bringing themselves to birth
In their own underworld,
The dark, dark space

Of deaths and renewals.
The cat keeps an eye on it.
Nettles protect it.
Everything goes through there.

QATAR

A transit lounge, in Nineteen Eighty One—
I doze all night on a rickety chair
In God's own country, where the biblical wars
Have still to happen. A cold sun,

A muezzin call, a man on a prayer-strip
At the dry-goods warehouse
Out by the runway. Sheds, a fuel stop—
And soon our wretched crew will reappear

From humping each other, in the First Class Hotel.
I put aside Merton's Elected Silence,
Learning to sit still.
Doha, Doma, what's the difference,

And what do they do here anyway,
Where objects are weightless
In Duty Free days, and everyone seems to pray?
Years later, Bartholomew's Atlas

Makes it all clear, through the magnifying glass
Of Armageddon—one vast aircraft carrier
Catapulting planes into abstract space—
Where now, a goat grazes,

And pearlfishers dive between two dimensions
And what I would kill for is that single flyblown Coke.
I open Merton again, just to keep awake.
I have not been paying attention.

They were born, the daughters of Lot,
Facing the wrong direction.
A cart was loaded, a donkey stolen—
Now they cling to their Father,
Not looking back. Behind them
The site of disaster,
Immemorial. Meteor-showers
Bloom like rockets, magnesium flares
In an underlit sky. Benighted
The city burns, its merchant houses—
Buy if there's a run, but otherwise wait—
Settling, like silt, in the dregs of a harbour
Clogged with shipwrecks, while the fleet,
Offshore, of the new administrators,
Stays for surrender.
                              There they go,
The pair of them, and the one man in their life,
Through a hole blown in the cliff
Called Mother, her salt profile
Staring backwards, into the time before birth—
Baby, I never loved you. Make my day
And pack your bags . . . —a hole big enough
For a motorway, if there were still petrol,
And cars were for more than sleeping in,
And speeds outran the Bible.

They have eyes, now, for the present only.
Bacchanalia reigns. Smashed amphorae,
Scattered rations. Drunks beneath the jesse tree
On the last of their own good wine.
The founding of houses, the birth of children—
Now, it will never happen.
Their father, instead, is their husband.
Sodomites and sodomised,
They are breaking bread together.

THE PLEASURE THERMOMETER

You would have it made of strong metal,
The pleasure thermometer—strong, strong metal,
The better to descend, like a bathyscaph,
Beyond fahrenheit and centigrade,
Through the mind-darkening elements, the ecstasies,
Measuring them coldly, before they destroy you.

Which orifice, then, to allow it?
Which air to hang it out in?
Under the lymph-nodes, between the thighs,
Where the fevers dwell? The undersides of tongues,
The insides of many mouths, have felt it.
Smashed, the mercury runs beneath hundreds of beds,

Escaping forever. Held to the light, though,
Drawn from its sleeve, inserted
Into the living moment, it will bring back something—
Cries in the night. The finest, never sold,
Are for liquid gold molasses, molten sugar-fires
That crystallise, grown cold.

In the far north, wheat is being sown,
In the far south, rice. Today, by royal decree,

Is Planting Day, and the Day of the Dead.
I see my mother, deep in the Tang Dynasty,

Obedient at the wellhead, with the other widows
Whose husbands have gone before them,

Filling buckets, staggering on bandaged legs
Up the gravel paths, to the overgrown plots.

Arthritically, they deadhead and they seed.
Bray Head, the Wicklow Mountains all around them,

Clarify fantastically, in the blue April air.
But the great perspectives are not their business—

Today is Qing Ming, or Pure Brightness Day.
They have travelled, the widows,

Through Chinas of the mind—old wars, dispersions,
Where the womb empties, the hair grows grey—

To be here today, in a place of loyalty, kindness.
I watch them, from my great remoteness,

Through a veil of space and time,
Paying the keeper of graves, for another year.

A train goes by, from Wexford up to Dublin—
Gulls, the coastline. None of them hear it—

Earth, their precious Emperor has told them,
Is realer than ashes scattered far at sea.

SELF-PORTRAIT IN A STEEL SHAVING MIRROR

Keith Douglas 1920–1944

All night, you rumble into your battle station—
Eros versus Death. The men play patience,
Know nothing. Who could sleep
In a desert strewn with phallic prototypes

Deflowered out of nowhere? Opiates—
Morphine, quinine—squat on the gunner's shelf
By the shaving mirror. Stare at your self
And watch a human being disintegrate

In the wolf hour before morning—one part love
And one part nothingness,
The front line in between, the crossing over

All blacked out, and the vastness of no-man's land
Swallowing all those women once undressed
Who led you on, with the enemy behind you.

Notebook Five

McCRYSTAL'S

All night, on the opposite shore,
The lights of McCrystal's glitter.
You could walk on water
To get there, and be drowned,
Or take the long way round,

Where a million instants
Shatter and die on the windscreen—
Late summer insects, flecks of rain
Melting into each other again—
And change is the only constant.

There, where sky and water meet
And none are strangers to themselves
Or the land beneath their feet,
McCrystal, quietly stacking shelves,
Open infinitely late

On the universe, picks you out
From the fixed and wandering stars
Of sailmakers' cottages, nightbound cars
Forever approaching, the only man
Driven by supernatural doubt.

Everything mortal shies away.
The horse in foal, and the fox
Dead in your headlights, oozing blood,
Glittering back an evil eye,
You too, my friend, will have to die . . .

And the goddesses, the gods
Of summer—girls, bare-midriffed,
Riding shotgun through the moonroofs,
Running the double gauntlet
Of boyfriends and the temperance squad.

The forecourt of his filling station
Blazes like broad daylight.
Ask—have you travelled all this way
Past trees and people, gable ends
Turning black on a western sky

To cash a cheque? Or shatter the veil
Of phenomena? His Holy Grail
Is sand and futures, factory-floors,
Grazing rights on an airfield
Overgrown since the last World War. . . .

Everything everyone needs he stores,
As self-contained as a man-god
In the aftermath of creation.
Anything else, from the farther shore,
Is optical, an illusion.

WINDHOEK

You would go there, just to follow a name,
And find nothing. No, not nothing, a city
Of half a million, a little history
In a desert. And the Irish who came,

O'Hagans and O'Donoghues, running bars
On Main Street. Like yourself, no longer afraid
Of words like *alien, rootless, void,*
Vertiginous, in the high blue African air.

You who deal in crystals, self-reflection,
Do well here. Who think in aeons,
Asteroid fallout, shattered mammoth bones

Of your own Kalahari, passing through,
Panhandling, huge perspectives
In your eyes, and the ghost towns you outgrew.

BIRTHRIGHT

Her hips swung open like a gate.
New life broke through, to the great field
Of the future. We were waiting
Already, the rest of us.
With our headstart and our grazing rights
From heaven. The long perspectives
Still held water.

And there it stood, the very first house.
Who owned it now? An uncle,
Doting, looked through the one bay window,
A lifelong student of local jades
And pages of racing form.
Grey as ghosts, in the sunken garden,
Carp were blooming,

Pondlife coming through.
History would learn to forget itself
In these low-level seethings,
Tassel and stalk, and the scattering of crows
At the blast of a barley-gun
Doing its own work, keeping its vigil
Into the marches of long ago.

Our summers, vast and terrible now,
Wait for the new inheritor,
She who was cut from her mother's womb
In a forest of stirrups, drips and singing bottles,
Half milk-yield, half blood-sample.
No hips, no gate. In place of truth,
Her stakehold on myth.

These are not my people. Who, then,
Do I drive towards, as the African afternoon,
Black into yellow and back again,
Blinks once, blinks twice, before the oncoming Rains?

Our table was a water table,
Now I know. Eating, we floated—
At a slight list, when Father was on the bottle,
But dignified, silent. Our tree of roots,

Too, had a civil war town
In its shadow, restless daughters,
Stepmothers. It, too, seemed to hang upside down
On the skyline, its branches all water,

Like this one I drive towards
Time out of mind, through the orphaned, the estranged,
That blackens, grows enormous
As the war-zones change.

THE BAKER

My husband was a baker
And made these. The lemon tarts,
Eclairs, the cream confections
And the dreamy farls.

You may have seen him, any day,
Through the street window
Slaving, stripped to the waist
Or wearing his long white apron

In the body heat of ovens,
Floury trays—an artisan.
His hours were long. He lived,
Invisibly for the most part,

At the back of his own creations.
That he drank champagne
Each night, by the magnum,
Ought not to surprise you.

That he ran away
In childhood, broke the mould.
And served his long apprenticeship
On the road, with the journeymen.

I, who kept the front of the shop
Where his passion cooled
Into flans, strawberry gateaux
And a string of grand-children

Ask that he be remembered
Whose light burned late and early,
Whose hours were strange
And whose cakes were his afterlife.

THE BLACK BOOK

About the terrible politics of this island
Let us educate ourselves anew. Hand it to me,
The black book you were reading, with the names,
The negotiations, the graves dug up

In the lonely places, bogs and border marches,
And the executioners, doing time
In the open prison of their own kitchens,
Reminiscing, over hot strong cups of tea.

The names, of course, are changed, and the places
Falsified. Where X met Y
One ancient day, to seal the fate of Z,
Is a grey zone of compromise now,

Or call it a housing estate. I grew up next door
To murder. You combed your hair
With soldiers in the mirror, closing in.
Let us not argue then, on the lesser points,

But hand me the little black book, with the names, the places,
Like a lost undersea continent
Rising forever, to rediscover itself
In our own eyes, and call itself Ireland.

About the goldfinch
Everyone knows,
And the one self-portrait
Traded for horseflesh.

Poor maker, blown away
When the Delft magazine
Exploded, forgive yourself
The limits of art.

Eight canvases
Stretched on nothingness,
Fraying . . . Your self-employed
Signature on the void.

Wood is a ledge to perch on—
A bird, a moment—
And your face, against heaven,
Unmakes itself, in layers.

Is suddenly inside you, like a radium trace—
And the winter woods, the city below,
Are unfinished business, in the light of other days.
You stand and listen. A hooded crow
Flaps out of nowhere, croaks and settles,
Spooking the immemorial forest floor.
Millions of dead souls underfoot, dry and brittle,
Wait to be chosen. You have been here before,
One of the revenants. God knows when,
In search of himself, who gets it wrong again

And finds himself wandering, generations later,
In the same dark wood. . . . Unliving
You see into life, from a great way off—
But where is the ground of knowledge, self-belief?
A tennis ball left by a walker's dog, between states,
Waylays you. A boy in search of savagery
Taps in a glade, on his little skin drum.
And far away, that nineteenth-century thrumming
Is trains on viaducts. . . . Ethereal, unbelonging,
Attaching yourself to any and everything,

You wander through births and deaths. An orphanage
Shelters you, a house for the dying.
You warm your hands at the spirit of every age.
And now, in the depths of winter, getting by
On objects, passing strangers, flight-paths, dogs,

On moments of absolute stillness, you draw breath,
Casting about for anyone to work with.
The king hunting boar, the railwayman with his grog
Have gone to ground. The woman, out of her head,
Who painted all night in a zeppelin shed

And gathered mushrooms here, died famous long ago.
This time around, as the temperature drops
And the city lights come on, it is down to you
To come, by accident, on the Holy Grail.
Last year's leaves are everywhere. Snowmelt drips
In the cold, and high above you, vapour trails
Disintegrate, like the written word in space.
Stoop through centuries, tie your lace,
And pick it up once more, the long-lost thread
Of time, tradition and the living dead.

CACCIAGUIDA

Through a blowback
In history, coat-trailing
Between his lines
And mine, Cacciaguida,

You stand before us naked,
Our common ancestor.
Your coat's gone yellow.
You talk of gas, the trenches

Running like a seam,
A wound, a maggoty swarm
Through the map of Europe
Split and sutured.

I balance on my knee
The sacred book. *E venni*
Dal martiro a questa pace—
Dante . . . Buses pass,

And Florence, city of cities
Rushes on, into declension—
Women in mirrors,
Sirens in the distance.

Who came back, demobbed
And brutalised, from the Great War,
Hating his own children,
Cacciaguida, before my time?

Now I live in a foreign city,
Lighting candles
To his name, in empty churches,
Studying public records.

Bread and salt are my portion
On the wooden stairs.
Everything has come true
As the book foretold.

AMONG THE INFINITIES

We call this space a yard
To contain it, our unit of measure,
Among the infinities.

Mood and happenstance
Loom like shadows. An ash tree
From a neighbouring field

Leans in, a weather-front hovers,
Creating depressions,
Changing lives.

Haltered overnight, the neighbour's cow
Drops dung, an after-sign
That all is not dreamt, imagined—

And in the morning, the widow
Pegs linen on a breeze
With millions of years behind it.

How tiny she seems, like the rest of us,
In this long exposure,
Satellite-high, that takes in everything

On an updraught of spirit—
The banked sheen
Of strobe-lit water into the distance,

Drained foreshores, cattle in shallows,
Other men's comings and goings
On the face of the earth.

We have all been away
And come back. The anchor in the shed
Lies rusting, the ship's wheel falls apart,

And still, our house is disputed.
The satellite flash will hang on the wall
When seeing is believing.

EVE OF MARRIAGE

Pull off the manhole cover
On the depths of winter
There, at the heart of the yard.

Bend to your own self-image
Twelve feet down,
And haul up water through it

Spilling, against your own weight,
Human, braced
For that purest of retrievals

Once every generation.
The birds flock in
Too late. Black ice and breadcrumbs,

Scattered oatmeal, there in the snow,
Are their Holy Grail.
And the shattering glimpse,

The bore-hole through to the infinite
Closes again, cold metal.
Let the wellhead sleep

Beneath oncoming years, an eyelid
On a child's subconscious.
Soon, a man will enter the house,

A widow pass away. Old matting, sacks,
The middle ground itself
Will hide it, as you straighten up

And make of yourself a fulcrum
Between new weights.
Do you see what spills through your hair

Months later, at the great unveiling,
Nobody's daughter, nobody's bride,
Time alone on your side?

THE MYSTIC MARRIAGE

The fountain is stopped now
That made its water-noise
Into the small hours. Years ago
You thought it was rain,

Now, you sleep through everything
With the window open—
Late night jazz, a couple quarrelling,
Headlights, one mosquito.

'It is three o'clock
In the morning. I am going
To the lovers' bridge
In white mist, without you ...'

I wake from that dream
Towards daybreak. You beside me
Still sleeping.
You were never a dawn person.

The fountain is on again.
Whole years have passed. And still
We have never left the south—
From which, if ever, each returns

Eternally changed, or not at all.
A white noise of swifts
Outside. Swallows sipping
Old dregs of misery—

The drained glass on the wooden table
Slowly filling with light.
And suddenly, a crash of bells
From Saint John of Malta

Hard by, and two flights down,
Approaching, lifting the spell,
A river of children's voices
Growing and growing, out of the future,

Pure annunciation. Just in time
I retrieve it, like a dream transcript—
Our mystic marriage. Something, at last,
Has earthed itself inside you.

Look at us now, from the vanished years—
   Paris between the wars.
Penelopes and Juliets, pimps and racketeers
Of sugar and tobacco. Boys and girls
With stars on their lapels, who sleep on straw
Like everyone else, and carry out the slops.
And who could deny we're equals, under a Law
Annihilating us all? Conformists, resisters,
You I would never abandon, my own soul-sister,
Drinking brassy water from the taps

Of Drancy, where time and space are the antechamber
   To our latest idea of eternity—
Trains going east in convoys, sealed and numbered,
To an unknown destination. *Pitchipoi*
As the wits describe it, after the Yiddish tale—
A village in a clearing, zlotys changed for francs,
Children at their books, the old and frail
Looked after, and the rest suspiciously blank
On the postcards drifting like dead leaves
Back from that other world we are asked to believe in.

Death is not absolute! Two and two make five!
   My poems will survive!
Why not fly in the face of reason and scream
As Shestov says? Unscramble the anagram
Of my real name, which now is mud,

And tell Jean Wahl and Bachelard, *bien pensants,*
I forgive them, as they stalk the corridors
Of the Sorbonne, and the pages of the *Cahiers du Sud.*
I forgive us all, for we know not who we are—
Irrational, fleeting, caught between wars,

Faking our own death, in thirteen nation-states,
    As the monies collapse
And the borders, all of us transmigrating
Like souls, through the neutral space on the map.
Athens and Jerusalem, Ulysses and the Wandering Jew—
There we all go, the living and the dead,
The one in the other. . . . Call us the Paris crowd,
Unreal, uprooted, spectres drifting through,
The ashes of our ancestors in suitcases,
Bound for Buenos Aires, bound for the New.

In the steamroom dissipatings, the bathhouse stink,
    As the people of the Book
Undressed themselves, I learned at last how to think.
I saw the shame and beauty, and I shook
At patriarchs' aged knees, the love-handles of hips
And womens' breasts, emerging, disappearing,
Standing, kneeling, waiting, finally stripped
Of civilisation—in their natural state.
At the heart of the orgy, I saw into the years
Beyond steam and faucets, to the real Apocalypse.

And now they tell me 'Hide your poems, wait—
    Somewhere in Nineteen Eighty
Readers will find you. . . .' I see a Paris street,
Old letterbox, a drop-zone for the infinite
In a leaf-littered hallway, where a publisher long ago
Went out of business, and a young man searches
In the sibylline mess and the overflow
For a few lost words—*my own soul-sister, my wife*
Till death us do part, in the Eastern Marches . . .
And that, my friends, will be the afterlife.